FILMS DIRECTED BY JOHN FORD (FILM GUIDE)

Books LLC®, Reference Series, Memphis, USA, 2011. ISBN: 9781155190464. www.booksllc.net. Copyright: http://creativecommons.org/licenses/by-sa/3.0/deed.en

Table of Contents

3 Bad Men	2
3 Godfathers	2
7 Women	3
A Fight for Love	4
A Gun Fightin' Gentleman	4
A Marked Man	4
A Woman's Fool	4
Ace of the Saddle	5
Action (1921 film)	5
Airmail (film)	5
Arrowsmith (film)	5
Bare Fists	6
Born Reckless (1930 film)	6
Bucking Broadway	7
By Indian Post	7
Cameo Kirby	7
Cheyenne's Pal	8
Cheyenne Autumn	8
December 7th (film)	8
Desperate Trails	9
Doctor Bull	9
Donovan's Reef	9
Drums Along the Mohawk	11
Flesh (1932 film)	12
Fort Apache (film)	13
Four Men and a Prayer	14
Four Sons	14
Gideon's Day (film)	14
Gun Law (film)	15
Hangman's House	15
Hearts of Oak (film)	16
Hell Bent	16
Hitchin' Posts	16
Hoodman Blind	16
How Green Was My Valley (film)	17
How the West Was Won (film)	18
Jackie (1921 film)	20
John Ford filmography	21
Judge Priest	21
Just Pals	24
Kentucky Pride	24
Lightnin'	25
Little Miss Smiles	25
Marked Men (1919 film)	25
Mary of Scotland (film)	25
Men Without Women (film)	26
Mister Roberts (1955 film)	26
Mogambo	28
Mother Machree	29
My Darling Clementine	29
Napoleon's Barber	31
North of Hudson Bay	31
Pilgrimage (1933 film)	31
Rider of the Law	31
Riders of Vengeance	31
Riley the Cop	32
Rio Grande (film)	32
Roped	33
Rustlers (film)	33
Salute (film)	33
Seas Beneath	34
Sergeant Rutledge	34
Sex Hygiene	34
She Wore a Yellow Ribbon	35
Silver Wings (film)	35
Stagecoach (1939 film)	36
Steamboat Round the Bend	38
Straight Shooting	38
Strong Boy	38
Submarine Patrol	39
Sure Fire	39
Thank You (1925 film)	39
The Adventures of Marco Polo	39
The Battle of Midway	40
The Big Punch	40
The Black Watch	40
The Blue Eagle	41
The Brat	41
The Craving (1918 film)	41
The Face on the Bar-Room Floor (1923 film)	41
The Fighting Brothers	42
The Fighting Gringo (1917 film)	42
The Fighting Heart (1925 film)	42
The Freeze-Out	42
The Fugitive (1947 film)	42
The Girl in Number 29	43
The Grapes of Wrath (film)	43
The Gun Packer	46
The Horse Soldiers	46
The Hurricane (1937 film)	47
The Informer (1935 film)	48
The Iron Horse (film)	49
The Last Hurrah (1958 film)	49
The Last Outlaw	50
The Long Gray Line	50
The Long Voyage Home	50
The Lost Patrol (1934 film)	51
The Man Who Shot Liberty Valance	52
The Outcasts of Poker Flat (1919 film)	54
The Phantom Riders	54
The Plough and the Stars (film)	55
The Prince of Avenue A	55
The Prisoner of Shark Island	55
The Quiet Man	56
The Rising of the Moon (film)	57
The Scarlet Drop	58
The Scrapper	59
The Searchers (film)	59
The Secret Man	62
The Shamrock Handicap	62
The Soul Herder	62
The Sun Shines Bright	62
The Tornado	63
The Trail of Hate	63
The Village Blacksmith (film)	63
The Wallop	64
The Whole Town's Talking	64
The Wings of Eagles	65
The World Moves On	65
They Were Expendable	66
Thieves' Gold	67
Three Jumps Ahead	67
Three Mounted Men	67
Tobacco Road (film)	67
Torpedo Squadron	68
Two Rode Together	68
Up the River	69
Upstream (film)	70
Wagon Master	70
Wee Willie Winkie (film)	71
What Price Glory? (1952 film)	72
When Willie Comes Marching Home	72
Wild Women	72
Women in Defense	73
Young Mr. Lincoln	73

Introduction

Purchase of this book entitles you to a free trial membership in the publisher's book club at www.booksllc.net. (Time limited offer.) Simply enter the barcode number from the back cover onto the membership form. The book club entitles you to select from hundreds of thousands of books at no additional charge. You can also download a digital copy of this and related books to read on the go. Simply enter the title or subject onto the search form to find them.

Each chapter in this book ends with a URL to a hyperlinked online version. Type the URL exactly as it appears. If you change the URL's capitalization it won't work. Use the online version to access related pages, websites, footnotes, tables, color photos, updates. Click the version history tab to see the chapter's contributors. Click the edit link to suggest changes.

A large and diverse editor base collaboratively wrote the book, not a single author. After a long process of discussion and debate, the chapters gradually took on a neutral point of view reached through consensus. Additional editors expanded and contributed to chapters striving to achieve balance and comprehensive coverage. This reduced the regional or cultural bias found in many other books and provided access and breadth on subject matter otherwise little documented.

3 Bad Men

3 Bad Men is a 1926 Western film directed by John Ford.

Cast
- George O'Brien as Dan O'Malley
- Olive Borden as Lee Carlton
- Lou Tellegen as Sheriff Layne Hunter
- Tom Santschi as 'Bull' Stanley
- J. Farrell MacDonald as Mike Costigan
- Frank Campeau as 'Spade' Allen
- Priscilla Bonner as Millie Stanley
- Otis Harlan as Editor Zach Little
- Phyllis Haver as Lily (prairie beauty)
- Georgie Harris as Joe Minsk
- Alec B. Francis as Rev. Calvin Benson (as Alec Francis)
- Jay Hunt as Nat Lucas (old prospector)
- Grace Gordon as Millie's pal (uncredited)
- George Irving as Gen. Neville (uncredited)
- Bud Osborne as Hunter's henchman (uncredited)
- Vester Pegg as Henchman shooting Lucas (uncredited)
- Walter Perry as Pat Monahan (uncredited)

Source (edited): "http://en.wikipedia.org/wiki/3_Bad_Men"

3 Godfathers

3 Godfathers is a 1948 American western film directed by John Ford and filmed (although not set) primarily in Death Valley. The screenplay, written by Frank S. Nugent and Laurence Stallings, is based on the novelette of the same name written by Peter Kyne. Ford had already adapted the film once before in 1919 as *Marked Men*. The original silent adaptation by Ford is thought to be lost today. The story is something of a re-telling of the story of The Three Wise Men in an American western context.

Plot
Cattle rustlers Robert Hightower, Pedro 'Pete' Rocafuerte, and William Kearney rob a bank in the town of Welcome, Arizona, but Kearney suffers a bullet wound and they have to flee into the desert, pursued by the posse of Sheriff Buck Sweet, who puts a bullet in their water bag. They eventually lose their horses in a desert storm and end up walking. In their search for water, they come across a water hole, which has, however, been destroyed by the misguided efforts of a bumbling tenderfoot. In his covered wagon left nearby lies his wife (actually the niece of Sheriff Sweet), who is very pregnant and about to give birth. With the help of the trio, she has a boy, whom she names Robert William Pedro after her benefactors. Before dying, she extracts a promise from the baby's three godfathers that they will take care of him. Moved by the woman's plight, the three desperados uphold their promise despite the acute lack of water.

With William wounded from the robbery and the sheriff's posse in pursuit, they leave with the baby for the town of New Jerusalem, which lies across a wide expand of desert. After crossing a salt flat, William dies from exhaustion and the effects of his injury; later, Pete falls and breaks his leg. Robert leaves him his pistol, for "protection from coyotes." As he walks away, he hears a single gunshot.

Finally at the end of his strength, Robert nearly loses hope, but in his delirium the ghosts of his two friends appear and refuse to let him give up. He finally reaches New Jerusalem and enters a cantina where people are singing Christmas carols, and then collapses right after Buck catches up with him. Robert is arrested, but because of his heroism and refusal to give up custody of his godson in favor of the Sweets (whom he has now befriended), he is viewed by the townspeople as a hero even before the trial comes to its conclusion. In the end, Robert is sentenced to the minimum sentence of a year and a day and, as he leaves to serve his sentence with a promise to return, is given a cordial farewell by the entire town.

Cast

- John Wayne as Robert Marmaduke Hightower
- Harry Carey Jr. as William Kearney "The Abilene Kid"
- Pedro Armendáriz as Pedro "Pete" Fuerte
- Mildred Natwick as Mother
- Ward Bond as Perley "Buck" Sweet
- Mae Marsh as Mrs. Sweet
- Jane Darwell as Miss Florie
- Guy Kibbee as Judge
- Hank Worden as Curley

Points of interest

This film was dedicated to John Ford's friend and early star, Harry Carey, whose son Harry Carey Jr. played one of the title roles. *Tokyo Godfathers* is partly based on this film.
Source (edited): "http://en.wikipedia.org/wiki/3_Godfathers"

7 Women

7 Women, also known as *Seven Women*, is a 1966 film drama made by MGM. It was directed by John Ford, produced by Bernard Smith and John Ford, from a screenplay by Janet Green and John McCormick, based on the story *Chinese Finale* by Norah Lofts. The music score was by Elmer Bernstein and the cinematography by Joseph LaShelle. This was the last feature film directed by Ford, ending a career which spanned over fifty years.

The film starred Anne Bancroft, Sue Lyon, Margaret Leighton, Flora Robson, Mildred Dunnock, Betty Field, Anna Lee, with Eddie Albert, Mike Mazurki and Woody Strode.

Plot

The story takes place in China in 1935 on a remote missionary post.

The mission, made up predominantly of women, is threatened from within as well as from outside. Everything is calm on the surface as the head of the mission, Miss Agatha Andrews (Margaret Leighton) runs things fairly rigidly, self-righteously believing her idea of Christian piety is the only correct way to live. The other women at the mission are Miss Argent (Mildred Dunnock), her loyal assistant; Miss Binns (Flora Robson) and Mrs. Russell (Anna Lee) from the nearby British mission, who are seeking safety from the war atrocities; Mrs. Florrie Pether (Betty Field), whose husband, Charles Pether (Eddie Albert) is a mission teacher and the only male there; Miss Ling (Jane Chang), the demure Chinese mission teacher and translator and Emma Clark (Sue Lyon), a member of the staff and the youngest girl at the mission.

Neurotic tension is brewing and Miss Andrews soon turns out to have a god complex, her crazed piety is nothing like the religion she claims to have practiced. She is obsessed in keeping Emma, her beloved project, from being "defiled". The arrival of an elegant, humanistic, cynical, agnostic doctor, Dr. Cartwright (Anne Bancroft), soon disrupts the fragile peace, especially when Emma becomes the doctor's admirer. Cartwright stands apart from the group of women and she and Andrews clash over Cartwright's attitude, her profane speech, her smoking, and her total lack of interest in participating in the daily if austere prayers. Florrie is pregnant but fears she is too old to give birth without problems. Cartwright has to deal with the pregnant woman giving birth in very primitive conditions, then a cholera outbreak, and finally an attack by Mongol marauders who commit atrocities, gross indignities, and acts of barbarism. She inspires the women to great bravery and they manage to cope with extremely dangerous situations, but in the end Cartwright is forced to offer herself up to the Mongol leader, Tunga Khan (Mike Mazurki), as a concubine to save the group. This sets a rift among the missionaries with Agatha appalled by Cartwright's decision, while Miss Binns applauds her courage and spirit. Each member of the group offers a different response to the danger, which gives the film a certain depth and diversity. In the end the roles seemed to have reversed, Cartwright becomes the selfless and determined savior, and Agatha the depraved self-righteous one of false religion. At the film's conclusion, Cartwright toasts her captor Tunga Khan with a poisoned cup of tea which he drinks and immediately keels over as she coldly utters: "So long ya bastard!" After a moment's hesitation, Cartwright herself drinks the poison and shatters the cup on the floor as the screen goes black.

As Ford was a devout Catholic, the film shows the difference between the claim of being moral and the act of morals; the stark contrast between compassion and sacrifice to the austere holier-than-thou philosophy.

Cast

- Anne Bancroft as Dr. D.R. Cartwright
- Sue Lyon as Emma Clark, Mission Staff
- Margaret Leighton as Agatha Andrews, Head of Mission
- Flora Robson as Miss Binns, Head of British Mission
- Mildred Dunnock as Jane Argent, Andrews' Assistant
- Betty Field as Mrs. Florrie Pether, Charles' pregnant wife
- Anna Lee as Mrs. Russell, Mission Staff
- Eddie Albert as Charles Pether, Mission Teacher
- Mike Mazurki as Tunga Khan, Bandit Leader
- Woody Strode as Lean Warrior
- Jane Chang as Miss Ling, Mission Staff
- Hans William Lee as Kim, Mission Staff
- H.W. Gim as Coolie
- Irene Tsu as Chinese Girl

Acclaim

Fred Camper, Richard Combs and Simon Galiero all rated it among the top ten greatest movies of all time. The film also appeared in several other lists. These include:

- Most Misappreciated American Films of All Time (1977, Andrew Sarris)
- Most Misappreciated American Films of All Time (1977, Pascal Bonitzer)
- Most Misappreciated American Films of All Time (1977, Serge Daney)
- Most Important American Films (1977, Erno Patalas)
- Most Important American Films (1977, Luc Moullet)
- Genre Favorites: Adventure (1993)
- Alternative Choices to Sight and Sound's 360 Films Classics List (1998)
- 100 Essential Films (2003–Present, Slant Magazine)
- Favorite Films (1975, Syndicat Francais de la Critique de Cinema)

Cahiers du cinéma voted it the 6th best film of 1966 and Andrew Sarris rated it the third-best of 1966 (only being beaten by Blow-up and Gertrud).

The film was voted by *They Shoot Pictures, Don't They?* as the 680th greatest films of all time, in a poll of 1,825 film critics, scholars, cinephiles, etc. and as well in a culmination of over 900 'greatest film' lists of all kinds, that were already existing.

Source (edited): "http://en.wikipedia.org/wiki/7_Women"

A Fight for Love

A Fight for Love (1919) is a Western film directed by John Ford and featuring Harry Carey. The film is considered to be lost.

Cast

- Harry Carey - Cheyenne Harry
- Joe Harris - Black Michael
- Neva Gerber - Kate McDougal
- Mark Fenton - Angus McDougal
- J. Farrell MacDonald - The Priest (as J. Farrel McDonald)
- Neola May - Indian Girl (as Princess Neola May)
- Chief John Big Tree
- Dark Cloud
- Edith Johnson
- Betty Schade

Source (edited): "http://en.wikipedia.org/wiki/A_Fight_for_Love"

A Gun Fightin' Gentleman

A Gun Fightin' Gentleman is a 1919 Western film directed by John Ford and starring Harry Carey. Because only three reels of originally five or six are believed to exist, this film is considered a partially lost film.

Cast

- Harry Carey - Cheyenne Harry
- J. Barney Sherry - John Merritt
- Kathleen O'Connor - Helen Merritt
- Harry von Meter - Earl of Jollywell (as Harry V. Meter)
- Lydia Yeamans Titus - Helen's Aunt (as Lydia Titus)
- Duke R. Lee - Buck Regan
- Joe Harris - Seymour
- John Cook - Old Sheriff (as Johnnie Cooke)
- Ted Brooks - The 'Youngster'

Source (edited): "http://en.wikipedia.org/wiki/A_Gun_Fightin%27_Gentleman"

A Marked Man

A Marked Man is a 1917 Western film directed by John Ford and featuring Harry Carey. The film is considered to be lost.

Cast

- Harry Carey - Cheyenne Harry
- Molly Malone - Molly Young
- Harry L. Rattenberry - Young (as Harry Rattenbury)
- Vester Pegg - Kent
- Anna Townsend - Harry's Mother (as Mrs. Townsend)
- William Steele - Sheriff (as Bill Gettinger)
- Hoot Gibson - Undetermined Role

Source (edited): "http://en.wikipedia.org/wiki/A_Marked_Man"

A Woman's Fool

A Woman's Fool is a 1918 Western film directed by John Ford featuring Harry Carey. The film is considered to be lost.

Cast

- Harry Carey - Lin McLean
- Betty Schade - Katie Lusk

- Molly Malone - Jessamine Buckner (as Mollie Malone)
- Millard K. Wilson - The Virginian
- Ed Jones - 'Honey' Wiggin
- Vester Pegg - Tommy Lusk
- William A. Carroll - Lusk
- Roy Clark - Billy
- Sam De Grasse - Undetermined Role

Source (edited): "http://en.wikipedia.org/wiki/A_Woman%27s_Fool"

Ace of the Saddle

Ace of the Saddle was a 1919 Western film directed by John Ford and featuring Harry Carey. The film is considered to be lost.

Cast

- Harry Carey - Cheyenne Harry Henderson
- Joe Harris - Sheriff, Yucca County
- Duke R. Lee - Sheriff Faulkner, Pinkerton County
- Viola Barry - Madeline Faulkner (as Peggy Pearce)
- Jack Walters - Inky O'Day
- Vester Pegg - Gambler
- William Courtright - Storekeeper (as William Cartwright)
- Zoe Rae - Child
- Howard Enstedt - Child
- Ed Jones - Bit Part (uncredited)

Source (edited): "http://en.wikipedia.org/wiki/Ace_of_the_Saddle"

Action (1921 film)

Action is a 1921 Western film directed by John Ford and featuring Hoot Gibson. It was based on Peter B. Kyne's popular novel *The Three Godfathers*. The film is considered to be lost. According to contemporaneous newspaper reports, *Action* was based on J. Allan Dunn's novel, *The Mascotte of the Three Star*; *Mascotte* appeared as the lead novel in the pulp magazine *Short Stories*, February 1921.

Cast

- Hoot Gibson - Sandy Brouke
- Francis Ford - Soda Water Manning
- J. Farrell MacDonald - Mormon Peters
- Buck Connors - Pat Casey
- Clara Horton - Molly Casey
- William Robert Daly - J. Plimsoll
- Dorothea Wolbert - Mirandy Meekin
- Byron Munson - Henry Meekin
- Charles Newton - Sherriff Dipple
- Jim Corey - Sam Waters
- Ed Jones - Art Smith (as Ed 'King Fisher' Jones)

Source (edited): "http://en.wikipedia.org/wiki/Action_(1921_film)"

Airmail (film)

Airmail is a 1932 adventure film directed by John Ford and starring Ralph Bellamy.

Cast

- Ralph Bellamy - Mike Miller
- Gloria Stuart - Ruth Barnes
- Pat O'Brien - Duke Talbot
- Slim Summerville - 'Slim' McCune (as 'Slim' Summerville)
- Lilian Bond - Irene Wilkins
- Russell Hopton - 'Dizzy' Wilkins
- David Landau - 'Pop'
- Leslie Fenton - Tony Dressel
- Frank Albertson - Tommy Bogan
- Hans Fuerberg - 'Heinie' Kramer
- Thomas Carrigan - 'Sleepy' Collins (as Tom Carrigan)
- William Daly - 'Tex' Lane

Source (edited): "http://en.wikipedia.org/wiki/Airmail_(film)"

Arrowsmith (film)

Arrowsmith is a 1931 film nominated for the Academy Award for Best Picture. It was written by Sidney Howard from the Sinclair Lewis novel *Arrowsmith*, and directed by John Ford.

Plot

An idealistic young medical student named Martin Arrowsmith (Ronald Colman) makes a favorable impression on Dr. Max Gottlieb (A. E. Anson). When Arrowsmith graduates, Gottlieb offers him a position as his research assistant, but the young man reluctantly has to turn him down. He has fallen in love with nurse Leora (Helen Hayes), and the salary is not enough to support the couple. Instead, he marries Leora and sets up his medical practice in her rural home town. One day, he develops a serum to cure a fatal cow disease ravaging the nearby herds. Reinvigorated, he decides to join Gottlieb at the McGurk Institute in New York. Meanwhile, Leora miscarries and, to the couple's sorrow, is unable to have any more children, so she devotes herself to supporting her husband's mission.

When there is an outbreak of bubonic plague in the West Indies, Gottlieb believes that Arrowsmith's experience with his cow serum would prove invaluable. Eager to help mankind, Arrowsmth goes to a Caribbean island to work with scientist Gustav Sondelius (Richard Bennett) in his struggle to save the natives. Leora accompanies him, despite his fear for her safety. Sir Robert Fairland (Lumsden Hare) refuses to let him give his serum to only half the people and give the other half a placebo in order to test the effectiveness of the cure. Howard University-educated Dr. Oliver Marchand (Clarence Brooks) offers them the people of his island as test subjects. Among the participants in the experiment is Mrs. Joyce Lanyon (Myrna Loy), a New Yorker stranded on the island who is attracted to Arrowsmith.

Sondelius contracts the disease; just before he dies, he pleads with Arrowsmith to save as many lives as possible by abandoning the scientific protocol. The young doctor becomes worried about his wife. He goes to see her, but too late; she too has succumbed to the plague. Arrowsmith then decides to give the serum to all, saving many lives.

On Arrowsmith's return to New York, Dr. Tubbs (Claude King), the head of the McGurk Institute, is eager to bask in his reflected glory. However, when Gottlieb suffers a stroke during the reception in Arrowsmith's honor, Arrowsmith decides to quit the institute and join his friend and co-worker Terry Wickett (Russell Hopton) in a makeshift lab doing real research.

Cast (in credits order)

- Ronald Colman as Dr Martin Arrowsmith
- Helen Hayes as Leora Arrowsmith
- Richard Bennett as Gustav Sondelius
- A.E. Anson as Professor Max Gottlieb
- Clarence Brooks as Oliver Marchand
- Alec B. Francis as Twyford
- Claude King as Dr Tubbs
- Bert Roach as Bert Tozer
- Myrna Loy as Mrs Joyce Lanyon
- Russell Hopton as Terry Wickett
- David Landau as State Veterinarian
- Lumsden Hare as Sir Robert Fairland - Governor

Production

The film is largely faithful to the novel, but completely omits all mention of Arrowsmith's wealthy, self-centered second wife. Myrna Loy has only a few scenes with Colman, and their relationship is undeveloped. According to Robert Osborne, host of Turner Classic Movies, Helen Hayes noted that various scenes were dropped from the script without explanation. It turns out that Samuel Goldwyn had hired director John Ford on condition that he not drink during the production. As a result (according to Osborne), Ford sped up the filming as much as he could.

Reaction

The film was a financial and critical success, garnering four Oscar nominations.

Source (edited): "http://en.wikipedia.org/wiki/Arrowsmith_(film)"

Bare Fists

Bare Fists is a 1919 Western film directed by John Ford and featuring Harry Carey. The film is considered to be lost.

Cast

- Harry Carey - Cheyenne Harry
- Betty Schade - Conchita
- Joe Harris - Boone Travis
- Vester Pegg - Lopez
- Mollie McConnell - Conchita's Mother (as Molly McConnell)
- Anna Mae Walthall - Ruby (as Anna May Walthall)
- Howard Enstedt - Bud
- Joseph W. Girard - Harry's Father (as Joseph Girard)

Source (edited): "http://en.wikipedia.org/wiki/Bare_Fists"

Born Reckless (1930 film)

Born Reckless is a 1930 American crime comedy directed by Andrew Bennison and John Ford written by Donald Henderson Clarke based on his novel Louis Beretti. The film starred Edmund Lowe and Catherine Dale Owen.

Plot

A gangster, Louis Beretti, gets caught involved in a jewelry heist and taken to see the judge. The war has begun and hoping to use the publicity to get re-elected, the judge offers Louis and his two buddies, the choice of going to jail, or signing up to fight in the war - if they prove themselves, he will throw away their arrests.

Louis makes it home from the war (one of his buddies was killed), and opens up a night club downtown that becomes very successful. His employees are former members of his gang, and he maintains contact with "Big", still a gangster.

Louis falls for the girlfriend of his buddy who was killed in the war, but she already has plans to marry. He tells her nevertheless, that if she ever needs him, she should call and he will come. When her baby is kidnapped (her husband is away), she does call for Louis and he realizes that the kidnapping has been done by "Big" and the gang. Louis goes to save the baby and confront those of the gang who have taken part in the kidnapping. Shots are exchanged.

After he returns the baby to his mother, Louis goes back to his nightclub where "Big" is waiting. They talk of old times though they realize they will need to shoot it out, which they do...

Cast

- Edmund Lowe as Louis Beretti
- Catherine Dale Owen as Joan Sheldon
- Frank Albertson as Frank Sheldon
- Marguerite Churchill as Rosa Beretti
- William Harrigan as Good News Brophy

- Lee Tracy as Bill O'Brien
- Warren Hymer as Big Shot
- Ilka Chase as High Society Customer At Beretti's
- Ferike Boros as Ma Beretti
- Paul Porcasi as Pa Beretti
- Joe Brown as Needle Beer Grogan
- Ben Bard as Joe Bergman
- Pat Somerset as Duke
- Eddie Gribbon as Bugs
- Mike Donlin as Fingy Moscovitz
- Paul Page as Ritzy Reilly
- Roy Stewart as District Attorney Cardigan
- Jack Pennick as Sergeant
- Ward Bond as Sergeant
- Yola d'Avril as French Girl

Release

The film premiered on 11 May 1930.
Source (edited): "http://en.wikipedia.org/wiki/Born_Reckless_(1930_film)"

Bucking Broadway

Bucking Broadway is a 1917 film by John Ford, probably his sixth feature film. Long thought to be lost, along with about 60 of Ford's 70 silent films, it was found in 2002 in the archives of the CNC (the French National Center for Cinematography) . It was subsequently restored and digitized: it can be seen here on the website of Europa Film Treasures.

Plot

On a ranch in Wyoming, one of the cowboys, Cheyenne Harry (Harry Carey), falls in love with his boss's daughter. But she decides to elope to the city with Captain Thornton, a wealthy visitor to the ranch. She quickly discovers that life in the city is not what she expected. Cheyenne, devastated by the loss of his fiancée, decides to go to the city to find her, and in the end rescues her from the grips of Captain Thornton and from the extravagant and decadent way of life in the city.

Cast

- Harry Carey - Cheyenne Harry
- Molly Malone - Helen
- L. M. Wells - Her Father
- Vester Pegg - Thornton
- William Steele - Foreman (as William Gettinger)
- Gertrude Astor - Gladys (uncredited)
- Martha Mattox - Shocked Customer in Store (uncredited)

Source (edited): "http://en.wikipedia.org/wiki/Bucking_Broadway"

By Indian Post

By Indian Post is a 1919 short Western silent film directed by John Ford. One of the two reels survive.

Cast

- Pete Morrison - Jode MacWilliams
- Duke R. Lee - Pa Owens
- Magda Lane - Peg Owens
- Edward Burns- (as Ed Burns)
- Jack Woods - Dutch
- Harley Chambers - Fritz
- Hoot Gibson - Chub
- Jim Moore - Two Horns
- Jack Walters - Andy
- Otto Myers - Swede
- Ed Jones - Stumpy

Source (edited): "http://en.wikipedia.org/wiki/By_Indian_Post"

Cameo Kirby

Cameo Kirby is a 1923 drama film directed by John Ford and featured Jean Arthur in her onscreen debut. It was Ford's first film credited as John Ford instead of Jack Ford. It was based on a play by Booth Tarkington and Harry Leon Wilson. The story had been filmed as a silent before in 1915 with Dustin Farnum, who had originated the role on Broadway in 1909. The film was remade as an talking musical film in 1930.

Prints of the film exist in the UCLA Film and Television Archive and at the Cinemateca Portuguesa (Portuguese Film Archive), in Lisbon.

Cast

- John Gilbert - Cameo Kirby
- Gertrude Olmstead - Adele Randall
- Alan Hale - Colonel Moreau
- Eric Mayne - Colonel Randall
- W. E. Lawrence - Tom Randall (as William E. Lawrence)
- Richard Tucker - Cousin Aaron Randall
- Phillips Smalley - Judge Playdell
- Jack McDonald - Larkin Bunce
- Jean Arthur - Ann Playdell
- Eugenie Forde - Madame Davezac
- Frank Baker (uncredited)
- Ken Maynard (uncredited)
- Ynez Seabury (uncredited)

Source (edited): "http://en.wikipedia.org/wiki/Cameo_Kirby"

Cheyenne's Pal

Cheyenne's Pal is a 1917 Western film directed by John Ford and featuring Harry Carey. The film is considered to be lost.

Production

Filming took place over a three-day period (May 23-25, 1917) under the working titles *Cactus My Pal* and *The Dumb Friend*. The finished film was released by Universal Studios as a 20-minute silent film on two reels. The film is part of the "Cheyenne Harry" series of film featurettes, and was initially released as a promotional tool for the sale of USA war bonds during World War I.

Plot

Cheyenne Harry gets drunk and sells Cactus, his faithful horse (played by Pete Carey in full horse costume). Consumed with regret, he takes a job aboard the ship where Cactus is kept and the two escape in a midnight jump overboard.

Cast

- Gertrude Astor - Girl from dancing hall
- Harry Carey - Cheyenne Harry
- Pete Carey - Cactus
- Jim Corey - Noisy Jim
- Hoot Gibson - Cowboy
- Ed Jones - Cowboy
- Vester Pegg - Cowboy
- Steve Pimento - Cowboy
- William Steele (as Bill Gettinger) - Cowboy

Source (edited): "http://en.wikipedia.org/wiki/Cheyenne%27s_Pal"

Cheyenne Autumn

Cheyenne Autumn is a 1964 western starring Richard Widmark, Carroll Baker, James Stewart, and Edward G. Robinson. The film was the last western to be directed by John Ford, who proclaimed it an elegy for the Native Americans who had been abused by the American government and misinterpreted by many of the director's own films. With a budget of more than four million, the epic film was relatively unsuccessful, failing to earn a profit for its distributor, Warner Bros.

Cheyenne Autumn was photographed in Super Panavision 70 by William H. Clothier, whose work was nominated for an Academy Award. Gilbert Roland earned a Golden Globe Award nomination for Best Supporting Actor.

The original version was 158 minutes, Ford's longest work. Warner Brothers later decided to edit the "Dodge City" sequence out of the film, reducing the running time to 145 minutes, although it was shown in theatres during the film's initial release. This sequence features James Stewart as Wyatt Earp, and Arthur Kennedy as Doc Holliday. Some critics have argued that this comic episode, mostly unrelated to the rest of an otherwise serious movie, breaks the flow of the story. It was later restored for the VHS and subsequent DVD releases.

Much of the film was shot in Monument Valley Tribal Park on the Arizona-Utah border, where Ford had filmed scenes for many of his earlier films, especially *Stagecoach* and *The Searchers*. Although the principal tribal leaders were played by Ricardo Montalban and Gilbert Roland (as well as Dolores del Río and Sal Mineo in major roles), Ford again utilized numerous members of the Navajo tribe in this production.

Plot

In 1878, chiefs Little Wolf (Ricardo Montalban) and Dull Knife (Gilbert Roland) lead over three hundred starved and weary Cheyenne from their reservation in the Oklahoma territory to their home in Wyoming. The government sees this as an act of rebellion, and the sympathetic Captain Thomas Archer (Richard Widmark) is forced to lead his troops in an attempt to stop the tribe. As the press misrepresents the native's motives and goals for their trek as malicious, Secretary of the Interior Carl Schurz (Edward G. Robinson) tries to prevent violence from erupting between the army and the natives. Also featured are James Stewart as Wyatt Earp, Dolores del Río as "Spanish Woman" and Carroll Baker as a pacifist school teacher and Archer's (Widmark) love interest.

Source (edited): "http://en.wikipedia.org/wiki/Cheyenne_Autumn"

December 7th (film)

December 7th was a propaganda film produced by the US Navy and directed by John Ford in 1943, about the events of that date in 1941. As indicated by its title, the film was a presentation about the attack on Pearl Harbor, the event which sparked the Pacific War and American involvement in World War II generally.

The film begins with a chronological breakdown of the events of December 7, starting with the town of Honolulu gradually waking up and coming to life in the morning. A young private is credited with intercepting some vital information which his superiors dismiss; other sailors play baseball or attend religious services.

Then, "like locusts", the Japanese planes start humming over the air above Oahu, and begin the now infamous attack on American military installations on the island, including the sinking of the *Arizona*, and the bombing of Hickam Field. All the while, back in Washington, Japanese diplomats are still talking with Secretary of State Cordell Hull.

An animated sequence is then shown, with a large radio tower over Japan, broadcasting a fictional speech by Prime Minister Hideki Tojo. The narrator contradicts most of the "facts" that the Japanese leader tells his listeners in Tokyo, Kobe, and Okure.

After the attack Honolulu isn't quite the same; the island is put under martial law, barbed wire and other protective barriers are set up in case of invasion and even children have to be evacuated and given gas masks. The film is notable for its sympathetic depiction of the Japanese in Hawaii, and the difficulties they now had to go through.

Started within days of the attack, the original film was 82 minutes long and asked some embarrassing questions, such as why there was no long range reconnaissance and no short range air patrols. Further, the film had a lot of time devoted to the culture of the 160,000 Japanese in Hawaii and their response to the attack. For these reasons the long version of the film was censored for decades and the shorter 32 minute version released.

Awards

The film won an Academy Award in 1944 for Documentary Short Subject.
Source (edited): "http://en.wikipedia.org/wiki/December_7th_(film)"

Desperate Trails

Desperate Trails is a 1921 Western film directed by John Ford and featuring Harry Carey. The film is considered to be lost.

Cast

- Harry Carey - Bart Carson
- Irene Rich - Mrs. Walker
- George Stone - Dannie Boy
- Helen Field - Carrie
- Edward Coxen - Walter A. Walker
- Barbara La Marr - Lady Lou
- George Siegmann - Sheriff Price
- Charles Inslee - Doc Higgins (as Charles E. Insley)

Source (edited): "http://en.wikipedia.org/wiki/Desperate_Trails"

Doctor Bull

Doctor Bull (1933) is a comedy film directed by John Ford, based on the James Gould Cozzens novel *The Last Adam*. Will Rogers portrays a small town doctor who must deal with a typhoid outbreak in the community.

The film was well praised by the *New York Times*, which noted that the story is similar to Lionel Barrymore's film *One Man's Journey* when it premiered at the Radio City Music Hall in New York City. Andy Devine met his future wife during the making of this picture.

Cast

- Will Rogers - Dr. George 'Doc' Bull
- Vera Allen - Mrs. Janet 'Jane' Cardmaker, Widow of Charles Edward Cardmaker / Bull's Girlfriend
- Marian Nixon - May Tupping - Telephone Operator
- Howard Lally - Joe Tupping
- Berton Churchill - Herbert Banning - Janet's Brother
- Louise Dresser - Mrs. Herbert Banning
- Andy Devine - Larry Ward, Sodajerk
- Rochelle Hudson - Virginia (Muller) / Banning
- Tempe Pigott - Grandma Banning
- Elizabeth Patterson - Aunt Patricia Banning
- Nora Cecil - Aunt Emily Banning
- Ralph Morgan - Dr. Verney, Owner Verney Laboratory
- Patsy O'Byrne - Susan - Dr. Bull's Cook
- Veda Buckland - Mary - Janet's Maid
- Effie Ellsler - Aunt Myra Bull
- Helen Freeman - Helen Upjohn, New Winton Postmistress

Source (edited): "http://en.wikipedia.org/wiki/Doctor_Bull"

Donovan's Reef

Donovan's Reef is a 1963 American film starring John Wayne. It was directed John Ford and filmed on location on Kauai, Hawaii.

The cast included Elizabeth Allen, Lee Marvin, Dorothy Lamour, and Cesar Romero. The film marked the last time Ford and Wayne ever worked together on a project.

Synopsis

The film is a morality play in the guise of an action/comedy. It deals harshly (though not in an obvious way) with issues of racial bigotry, corporate connivance and greed, American beliefs of societal "superiority" and hypocrisy (i.e., the Boston shipping company considers carrying rum to be immoral, so they euphemistically refer to it as "West Indies goods").

Plot

The film begins with Thomas "Boats" Gilhooley (Marvin), an expatriate United States Navy veteran, working aboard a freighter. When he realizes that the ship he signed up for is just passing by Haleakaloha, French Polynesia, and not actually stopping there, he jumps ship to swim to the island.

Next, Michael "Guns" Donovan (Wayne), another expatriate U.S. Navy veteran and a former shipmate of Gilhooley, returns from a fishing trip aboard an outrigger canoe. Donovan is greeted by William "Doc" Dedham (Warden), the only physician in the archipelago, who is about to begin a one- or two-week pre-Christmas circuit of the "outer islands," taking care of the health needs of the residents. Dedham's three children are placed in Donovan's care.

The kids' plans for a peaceful celebration of Donovan's birthday, on December 7, are shattered by the arrival of Gilhooley, who shares the same birthday. There is an unbroken 21-year tradition that Donovan and Gilhooley have a knock-down, drag-out fight every birthday—to the delight of the local observers—and their 22nd year does not break the tradition. The two vets meet in (and trash) "Donovan's Reef," the saloon owned by Donovan.

John Wayne and Lee Marvin

Miss Amelia Dedham (Allen) is a "proper" young lady "of means" from Boston, who has become the chairman of the board of the Dedham Shipping Company. Her father is Doc Dedham, whom she has never met, but who now has inherited a large block of stock in the family company, making him the majority stockholder. She travels to Haleakaloha in hope of finding proof that Doc has violated an outdated (but still in effect) morality clause in the will which would enable her to keep him from inheriting the stock and retain control.

When word reaches Haleakaloha that Miss Dedham is on the way, a scheme is concocted by Donovan, Gilhooley, and the Marquis de Lage (Romero). De Lage is Haleakaloha's French governor, who hopes to find a post somewhere else. Donovan is to pretend to be the father of Doc's three *hapa* children (Leilani, Sarah and Luke), until Doc comes back and can explain things to the prim, proper Boston lady. The plan is reluctantly accepted by the oldest daughter, Leilani, who believes that the deception is because she and her siblings aren't white, a reflection of the bigotry of the period.

The plan works, and Amelia learns that her father, Donovan and Gilhooley were marooned on the Japanese-occupied island after their destroyer was sunk in World War II. With the help of the locals, the three men conducted a guerrilla war against the Japanese. She also learns that her father built a hospital, and lives in a large house (she had obviously expected to find a shack). A mystery develops, as she enters the house and sees a portrait of a beautiful Polynesian woman in royal trappings. This, the viewer understands, was Doc's wife, the mother of his children. Amelia is not told of the relationship, but she learns that the woman was named Manulani. Donovan mentions that Luke's mother (by implication, his own wife) had died in childbirth.

As the story develops, Amelia learns that life in the islands is not as she expected, and neither is Donovan, who proves to be educated and intelligent, and the owner of a substantial local shipping operation. Amelia, too, is not as expected, as when she strips off her outdated "swimming costume" to reveal a tight swimsuit, challenges Donovan to a swimming race, and dives into the water. They develop a truce, as de Lage tries to court Amelia (or rather, her $18,000,000).

When Dr. Dedham returns, father and daughter meet for the first time (Amelia: "Doctor Dedham, I presume?"). He has been told about the deception, and over dinner he explains that he was serving in World War II when his wife (Amelia's mother) died. When the war ended, he felt that he was not needed in Boston, but was desperately needed in the islands, so he stayed. He has even signed over his stock to Amelia, as he intends to remain in the islands. Just as he is about to explain about Manulani and their children (described by Amelia as "half-caste"), a hospital emergency interrupts.

It turns out that Manulani was the granddaughter of the last hereditary prince of the islands, and on Christmas Amelia finally puts all of the pieces together to solve the mystery. Leilani—Manulani's daughter—is not only the island's princess, but Amelia's sister, a relationship which is tearfully but joyfully acknowledged by both girls.

Amelia and Donovan evolve their truce into marriage plans. Gilhooley also finally marries his longtime girlfriend, Miss Lafleur (Dorothy Lamour). Donovan points out the new sign on the saloon, which is now "Gilhooley's Reef". Donovan has given the bar to his old shipmate as a wedding present.

Crisis resolved, life in the islands can return to normal.

Cast

- John Wayne as Michael Patrick "Guns" Donovan
- Elizabeth Allen as Amelia Dedham
- Lee Marvin as Thomas Aloysius "Boats" Gilhooley
- Jack Warden as Dr. William Dedham
- Cesar Romero as Marquis Andre de Lage, the French governor of the island
- Dorothy Lamour as Miss Lafleur, Gilhooley's sometime girlfriend
- Jacqueline Malouf as Lelani Dedham, Dr. Dedham's eldest daughter, hereditary ruler of the island
- Cherylene Lee as Sally Dedham, Dr. Dedham's younger daughter
- Jeffrey Byron as Luke Dedham, the

- Marcel Dalio as Father Cluzeot
- Mike Mazurki as the Police Constable

Production

While *Donovan's Reef* is set on the fictional island of Haleakaloha, which has a French governor, the only Polynesian language exhibited in the film is Hawaiian -- "Haleakaloha" can be translated as "Home of Laughter and Love" (hale = home, aka = laugh, aloha = love) -- and Amelia has come from Honolulu by sailing ship, indicating a location much closer to Hawaii than to French Polynesia.

The movie was actually filmed on Kauai, Hawaii. The home of the French island governor, the white beach house with coconut palms and surrounding grass lawn, is the Allerton Estate home and former summer residence of Hawaiian Queen Emma near Poipu Beach, now a part of the National Tropical Botanical Garden (without the scenes of boats and canoes on the Wailua River, which were edited and merged with scenes filmed at the Allerton Estate).

There is one major historical error: French Polynesia was 4,000 km (about 2200 nautical miles) east of the farthest Japanese expansion, and there was no fighting there.

In a bit of tongue-in-cheek, portraits of the founder and leaders of the Dedham Shipping Company are all of Warden (in appropriate period dress). The portrait of Manulani appears to be a similar treatment of Allen, as she would appear if she were Polynesian or *hapa*.

A mistaken use of a blasphemy slipped past the censors. At the end of the first fight between John Wayne and Lee Marvin, after Jack Warden has broken it up, Wayne and Marvin start to get out of the pond, but Marvin slipped and fell back into the water. As he did so, he exclaimed, "Jesus!" Because it was funny, the error was left in the film, and because the sound of the water partially obscured the exclamation, the dialogue was also left unaltered.

Critical reception

A.H. Weiler of the New York Times wrote that the movie was "sheer contrivance effected in hearty, fun-loving, truly infectious style". Variety called it an "effort-less effort", but praised the photography. Currently, the film has a rating of 60% on Rotten Tomatoes Source (edited): "http://en.wikipedia.org/wiki/Donovan%27s_Reef"

Drums Along the Mohawk

Drums Along the Mohawk is a 1939 historical Technicolor film based upon a 1936 novel of the same name by American author, Walter D. Edmonds. The film was produced by Darryl F. Zanuck and directed by John Ford. Henry Fonda and Claudette Colbert portray settlers on the New York frontier during the American Revolution. The couple suffer British, Tory, and Indian attacks on their farm before the Revolution ends and peace is restored. The film—Ford's first colour feature—was well received, was nominated for two Academy Awards and became a major box office success, grossing over US$1 million in its first year.

Plot

In 1776, American colonists Gilbert Martin (Henry Fonda) and Lana Borst (Claudette Colbert) marry and leave her luxurious home in Albany, New York for a small farm in Deerfield on the western frontier of the Mohawk Valley in central New York. Lana has difficulty in adjusting to frontier life, but soon is working alongside her husband.

The American Revolution begins. Lana is pregnant and miscarries when the Martin farm is burned to the ground in an Indian attack led by a Tory, Caldwell (John Carradine). With no home and winter approaching, the Martins accept work on the farm of wealthy widow Mrs. McKlennar (Edna May Oliver).

Life returns to peaceful normality; Mrs. McKlennar and the Martins prosper. However, an attack by Tories and Indians threatens the valley, and the militia is called up. Ill-equipped and poorly trained, the settlers barely manage to defeat the enemy at Oriskany. Gil returns home wounded and delirious. Lana is again pregnant, and while Gil recovers from his wounds, she gives birth to their son.

The Tories and Mohawks attack German Flatts, and the settlers take refuge in Fort Herkimer. Mrs. McKlennar is mortally wounded, and ammunition runs short. Gil makes a dash through enemy lines to secure help from nearby Fort Dayton. As the Indians scale the walls of the fort, reinforcements arrive from Fort Dayton. The Indians are overwhelmed. After the battle, the settlers learn the revolution has ended, and the American flag is unfurled above the fort.

Differences between film and novel

Of dramatic necessity, the film omits or neglects many of the book's characters and incidents, including the major plotline of John Weaver and Mary Reall. A notable variance from the novel's plot to film is the assignment of the "run" to Gil Martin, rather than to Adam Hartman, who appeared in the novel as the historical figure Adam Helmer, the frontiersman who executed the run in history. The Tory leader Caldwell is patterned after William Caldwell, who unlike in the dramatization, survived the conflict for another fifty years, and plays a far more prominent role than he did in the novel, where Walter Butler is the primary Tory figure. Many characters in the film, including Mrs. McKlennar, Christian Reall, Mrs. Demooth, and Joe Boleo, have fates diametrically opposite those of the novel. Boleo in particular, portrayed as a half-wit by Ford's brother Francis, is an important personage and godfather to Gil's second son. His fate in the film adaptation is that of a much more minor character in the novel.

Ford uses broad plot elements lifted from the novel to construct his story, but the film varies greatly in detail, tone, and focus from the novel. The personalities of many prominent characters are altered, and his plot compresses numerous events to fit within the time frame. While both film and novel focus on the development of Lana as a wife, in the novel she is the 18-year-old bride of a husband she has seen just six times. Colbert was twice that age when the movie was filmed, and her selection over Nancy Kelly to portray Lana leads to a complete rebuilding of the character, from a Mohawk Valley farm girl already experienced in hard work to a soft member of the gentry whose upbringing, not youth, is the source of her initial weakness and fears. Her family is actually killed in a raid in the novel.

In an early film scene, numerous neighbors and their families help Gil clear his land as a social event, then are forced to flee for their lives from a raid by "eight white men and a hundred Indians". The Martin cabin is burned and they lose everything. In the novel, Gil clears his own land, having only three neighbors, and while burning logs with two of them to clear the remaining trees, is forced to evacuate the pregnant Lana and their belongings by a raid of eight white men and six Indians. All four farms are burned out, as are two abandoned Tory houses in retaliation. This exaggeration by Ford typifies the heroic myth he seeks to create, whereas novelist Edmonds concentrated on depicting the everyday lives and relationships of the often less-than-heroic settlers, and the changes forced on their lives by an endless and baffling crisis. Unlike Edmonds, Ford uses humor throughout the script to establish a sympathetic quaintness and community at wide variance from the novel's theme. Moreover, in the novel the first major crisis in their marriage is neither Lana's fear of the frontier nor loss of their home, but the psychological trauma of miscarrying, which Ford totally ignores.

The Battle of Oriskany is a prominent part of Edmonds' novel but is not shown in the film. Ford planned to devote three weeks to filming the battle, but weather difficulties made following the shooting schedule impossible. Instead, he improvised the memorable scene in which Gil vividly describes the battle after returning to the McKlennar home.

Credited cast

- Henry Fonda — Gilbert "Gil" Martin
- Claudette Colbert — Magdelana "Lana" Martin
- Edna May Oliver — Mrs. McKlennar
- John Carradine — Caldwell
- Ward Bond — Adam Hartman
- Roger Imhof — Gen. Nicholas Herkimer
- Arthur Shields — Rev. Rosenkrantz
- Chief John Big Tree — Blue Back
- Francis Ford — Joe Boleo
- Jessie Ralph — Mrs. Weaver
- Robert Lowery — John Weaver
- Kay Linaker — Mrs. Demooth
- Russell Simpson — Dr. Petry
- Spencer Charters —Innkeeper

Critical reception

Frank S. Nugent reviewed the film for the *New York Times* of November 4, 1939 and wrote, "Walter D. Edmonds's exciting novel of the Mohawk Valley during the American Revolution has come to the...screen in a considerably elided, but still basically faithful, film edition bearing the trademark of Director John Ford...It is romantic enough for any adventure-story lover. It has its humor, its sentiment, its full complement of blood and thunder...a first-rate historical film, as rich atmospherically as it is in action...Mr. Fonda and Miss Colbert have done rather nicely with the Gil and Lana Martin...Miss Oliver could not have been bettered as the warlike Widow McKlennar...Mr. Shields's Rev. Rosenkrantz...Mr. Imhof's General Herkimer, Mr. Collins's Christian Reall, Spencer Charters's landlord, Ward Bond's Adam Helmer...They've matched the background excellently, all of them."

Academy Award nominations

The film was nominated for two awards: Best Supporting Actress (Edna May Oliver) and Best Cinematography (Ray Rennahan and Bert Glennon).
Source (edited): "http://en.wikipedia.org/wiki/Drums_Along_the_Mohawk"

Flesh (1932 film)

Flesh is a 1932 black-and-white drama film directed by John Ford (uncredited) and starring Wallace Beery as a German wrestler. Some of the script was written by Moss Hart and an uncredited William Faulkner.

Cast (in credits order)

- Wallace Beery as Polakai
- Ricardo Cortez as Nicky
- Karen Morley as Laura
- Jean Hersholt as Mr Herman
- John Miljan as Willard
- Herman Bing as Pepi - Head Waiter
- Vince Barnett as Karl - A Waiter
- Greta Meyer as Mrs Herman
- Edward Brophy as Dolan - A Referee

Trivia

- In the Coen brothers' film *Barton Fink*, (1991), the title character deals with writers' block while attempting to write a screenplay for a Wallace Beery wrestling picture. At the time they wrote it, the Coens were unaware of this movie. In addition, *Barton Fink* features a character based somewhat on William Faulkner that Fink consults for help in writing the script.

Source (edited): "http://en.wikipedia.org/wiki/Flesh_(1932_film)"

Fort Apache (film)

Fort Apache is a 1948 western film directed by John Ford and starring John Wayne and Henry Fonda. The film was the first of the director's "cavalry trilogy" and was followed by *She Wore a Yellow Ribbon* (1949) and *Rio Grande* (1950), both also starring Wayne. The story, which screenwriter James Warner Bellah based loosely on George Armstrong Custer and the Battle of Little Bighorn, as well as the Fetterman Massacre of 1866, was one of the first to present an authentic and sympathetic view of the Native Americans involved in the battle (Apache in the film, Sioux in the real battles).

The film was awarded the Best Director and Best Cinematography awards by the Locarno International Film Festival of Locarno, Switzerland.

Plot summary

After the American Civil War, highly-respected veteran Captain Kirby York (John Wayne) is expected to replace the outgoing commander at Fort Apache, an isolated U.S. cavalry post. York had commanded his own regiment during the Civil War and was well-qualified to assume permanent command. To the surprise and disappointment of the company, command of the regiment was given to Lieutenant Colonel Owen Thursday (Henry Fonda). Thursday, a West Point graduate, was a general during the Civil War. Despite his Civil War combat record, Lieutenant Colonel Thursday lacks experience with the Indians he is expected to oversee, and is an arrogant and egocentric officer.

Accompanying widower Thursday is his daughter, Philadelphia (Shirley Temple). She becomes attracted to Second Lieutenant Michael Shannon O'Rourke (John Agar), the son of Sergeant Major Michael O'Rourke (Ward Bond). The elder O'Rourke a recipient of the Medal of Honor as a major with the Irish Brigade during the Civil War, entitling his son to enter West Point and become an officer. However, the class-conscious Thursday forbids his daughter to see someone he does not consider a gentleman.

When there is unrest among the Indians, led by Cochise (Miguel Inclan), Thursday ignores York's advice to treat the natives with honor and to remedy problems on the reservation caused by corrupt Indian agent Silas Meacham (Grant Withers). Thursday's inability to deal with Meacham effectively, due to his rigid interpretation of Army regulations stating that Meacham is agent of the United States government and therefore entitled to Army protection (despite his own personal contempt for the man), coupled with Thursday's prejudicial and arrogant ignorance regarding the Apache drives the Indians to rebel. Eager for glory and recognition, Thursday orders his regiment into battle on Cochise's terms, a direct charge into the hills, despite York's urgent warnings that such a move would be suicidal. Thursday relieves York and orders him to stay back, replacing him with Captain Sam Collingwood (George O'Brien).

By deliberately misinterpreting his orders York spares the younger O'Rourke from battle. Thursday's entire command is nearly wiped out, but a few soldiers manage to escape back to the ridge where Captain York is positioned. Thursday himself survives but then returns to die with the last of his trapped men. Cochise spares York and the rest of the detachment because he knows York to be an honorable man.

Subsequently, now Lieutenant-Colonel Kirby York commands the regiment. Meeting with correspondents, he introduces Lt. O'Rourke, now married to Philadelphia Thursday. A reporter asks Colonel York if he has seen the famous painting depicting "Thursday's Charge." York, about to command a new and arduous campaign to bring in the Apaches, while believing that Thursday was a poor tactician and foolhardedly led a suicidal charge, says it is completely accurate and then reminds the reporters that the soldiers will never be forgotten as long as the regiment lives.

Production

Some exteriors for the film's location shooting were shot in Monument Valley, Utah. The exteriors involving the fort itself and the renegade Indian agent's trading post were filmed at the Corriganville Movie Ranch, a former Simi Hills movie ranch that is now a regional park in the Simi Valley of Southern California.

In the ball scene Col. Thursday dances while the band plays the tune of "Oh, Dem Golden Slippers", a minstrel song which was written in 1879, after the film was probably set.

Cast

- John Wayne as Capt. Kirby York
- Henry Fonda as Lt. Col. Owen Thursday
- Ward Bond as Sgt. Major Michael O'Rourke
- Shirley Temple as Miss Philadelphia Thursday
- John Agar as Lt. Michael Shannon "Mickey" O'Rourke
- Dick Foran as Sgt. Quincannon
- Pedro Armendariz as Sgt. Beaufort
- Miguel Inclan as Cochise
- Victor McLaglen as Sgt. Festus Mulcahy
- Guy Kibbee as Capt. Dr. Wilkens
- Anna Lee as Emily Collingwood
- George O'Brien as Capt. Sam Collingwood
- Jack Pennick as Sgt. Daniel Schattuck
- Irene Rich as Mary O'Rourke
- Grant Withers as Silas Meacham
- Movita as Guadalupe, Col. Thursday's cook
- Ray Hyke as Lt. Gates, an Adjutant

Source (edited): "http://en.wikipedia.org/wiki/Fort_Apache_(film)"

Four Men and a Prayer

Four Men and a Prayer is a 1938 adventure film directed by John Ford.

Cast
- Loretta Young - Miss Lynn Cherrington
- Richard Greene - Geoffrey Leigh
- George Sanders - Wyatt Leigh
- David Niven - Christopher Leigh
- C. Aubrey Smith - Col. Loring Leigh
- J. Edward Bromberg - Gen. Torres
- William Henry - Rodney Leigh
- John Carradine - Gen. Adolfo Arturo Sebastian
- Alan Hale - Mr. Furnoy
- Reginald Denny - Capt. Douglas Loveland
- Berton Churchill - Mr. Martin Cherrington
- Barry Fitzgerald - Trooper Mulcahay
- Claude King - Gen. Bryce
- Cecil Cunningham - Piper
- Frank Dawson - Manders

Source (edited): "http://en.wikipedia.org/wiki/Four_Men_and_a_Prayer"

Four Sons

Four Sons (1928) is a silent drama film directed and produced by John Ford and written for the screen by Philip Klein from a story by I. A. R. Wylie. It is one of only a handful of survivors out of the more than fifty silent films that Ford directed between 1917 and 1928. It starred Margaret Mann, James Hall, and Charles Morton. The film is also notable for the presence of the young John Wayne in an uncredited role as an Officer.

Plot

Mother Bernle is a widow in Bavaria with four sons: Franz, Johann, Andreas and Joseph.

Joseph receives a job offer from the United States, and he is given money to travel there by his mother.

The First World War is heating up. Franz, who is already serving in the German army, is joined by first Johann and then Andreas who is forced into the army after the village learns that Joseph joined the American army. Franz and Johann are killed on the eastern front. After Andreas is forced into the army, he is wounded on the western front and dies in his brother Joseph's arms.

In America, Joseph has married and is running a delicatessen. when America enters the war, Joseph enlists to fight for the American side. This causes problems for Mother Bernle, who is shunned in her village.

Cast
- Margaret Mann as Mother Bernle
- James Hall as Joseph 'Dutch' Bernle
- Charles Morton as Johann Bernle
- Ralph Bushman as Franz Bernle
- George Meeker as Andreas Bernle
- June Collyer as Annabelle
- Earle Foxe as Maj. von Stomm
- Albert Gran as The postman
- Frank Reicher as The schoolmaster
- Archduke Leopold of Austria as a captain
- John Wayne as Officer (uncredited)

Source (edited): "http://en.wikipedia.org/wiki/Four_Sons"

Gideon's Day (film)

Gideon's Day is a 1958 British crime film directed by John Ford and starring Jack Hawkins, Dianne Foster and Cyril Cusack. An adaptation of John Creasey's novel of the same name it is the first film to feature the character George Gideon of Scotland Yard, here played by Jack Hawkins. A police procedural, the film was directed by John Ford. The film's American title was *Gideon of Scotland Yard*.

Synopsis

The film follows a day in the life of a Metropolitan Police Officer George Gideon who receives information that one of his officers has been on the take, and he is forced to suspend him. When he hears that the same officer has been killed in an accident shortly afterwards, his interest is aroused, and he begins to investigate.

Cast
- Jack Hawkins - Detective Chief Inspector George Gideon
- Dianne Foster - Joanna Delafield
- Cyril Cusack - Birdy Sparrow
- Andrew Ray - PC Simon Farnaby-Green
- Anna Massey - Sally Gideon
- James Hayter - Robert Mason
- Howard Marion-Crawford - Chief Constable
- Laurence Naismith - Arthur Sayer
- Derek Bond - Detective Sergeant Kirby
- Miles Malleson - Judge
- John Le Mesurier - Prosecuting Counsel
- Robert Raglan - Dawson
- Michael Trubshawe - Sergeant Golightly
- Jack Watling - Reverend Small

Source (edited): "http://en.wikipedia.org/wiki/Gideon%27s_Day_(film)"

Gun Law (film)

Gun Law is a 1919 short Western film directed by John Ford.

Cast
- Pete Morrison - Dick Allen
- Helen Gibson - Letty
- Hoot Gibson - Bart Stevens, aka Smoke Gublen
- Jack Woods - Cayuse Yates
- Otto Myers - Gang Member
- Harry Chambers - Gang Member
- Ed Jones - Gang Member

Source (edited): "http://en.wikipedia.org/wiki/Gun_Law_(film)"

Hangman's House

Hangman's House is a 1928 romantic drama genre silent film set in Co. Wicklow, Ireland, directed by John Ford (uncredited) with intertitles written by Malcolm Stuart Boylan. It is based on a novel by Brian Oswald Donn-Byrne. It was adapted by Philip Klein with scenarios by Marion Orth. The film is also notable for containing the first confirmed appearance by John Wayne in a John Ford film.

Plot

Victor McLaglen as the film's heroic figure Hogan.

While stationed in Algiers Commandant Denis Hogan (Victor McLaglen) receives a letter containing bad news and requests that he be allowed to return to his home country of Ireland, where he is a wanted man. In Ireland, Baron James O'Brien (Hobart Bosworth) is told by his doctor that he has no more than a month to live. He decides to marry off his only daughter Connaught (June Collyer) to a socialite, John D'Arcy (Earle Foxe) despite her love of childhood friend Dermot McDermot (Larry Kent).

Hogan returns to Ireland and disguises himself as a holy man. On his way to the O'Brien's house he is recognised by a gatekeeper, whom he reveal his intentions to kill a man to. Hogan meets Dermot McDermot and the three men witness the lights of Glenmalure's chapel being lit, signifying a wedding is taking place. At this time a group of soldiers ask the gate keeper if he has seen Hogan. Later that night, after Connaught and D'Arcy have been wed, the Baron dies. On the night of his funeral Hogan sneaks about the grounds of Hangman's House and is spotted by D'Arcy. D'Arcy is startled by the appearance of Hogan. At bedtime D'Arcy tries to sleep with Connaught but she rejects his advances.

Larry Kent (left) and June Collyer (right) as the film's romantic couple.

A community race is held on St. Stephen's Day and Connaught's horse The Bard is due to race. The horse's jockey goes missing just before the race because of interference from D'Arcy who has bet against the horse. Dermot is required to jockey the horse and he wins the race leading a drunken D'Arcy to shoot The Bard. D'Arcy is ostracised by the community because of this. Hogan is arrested at the race. At night Dermot and D'Arcy meet in a pub where D'Arcy reveals that he had an affair with Hogan's sister. Dermot gives D'Arcy money to leave Ireland and threatens him that if he ever sees him again he will kill him.

Hogan escapes from prison and a gunfight erupts between his men and the guards. Later Dermot and Connaught visit Hogan's hideout and Hogan reveals that his sister died following D'Arcy's desertion. Connaught returns to Hangman's House to discover that D'Arcy has returned. After a struggle she flees to Dermot's house. Hogan and Dermot go to Hangman's House and confront D'Arcy. During a fight between the men a fire breaks out and burns down the house. Hogan and Dermot escape but D'Arcy falls to his death as a balcony collapses. Connaught and Dermot see Hogan off at the port as he returns to Algiers. Connaught gives Hogan a kiss and Dermot shakes his hands and thanks him. Connaught and Dermot walk away together as Hogan watches them.

Cast
- Victor McLaglen - Citizen Denis Hogan
- June Collyer - Connaught 'Conn' O'Brien
- Earle Fox - John D'Arcy
- Larry Kent - Dermot McDermot
- John Wayne - Horse Race Spectator/Condemned Man in Flashback (uncredited)
- Brian Desmond Hurst - Horse Race Spectator and witness to the horse shooting

Production

The film began production in January 1928 and took seven weeks to film.

Reception

The film received positive reviews, Wilfred Beaton of Film Spectator called it "the finest program picture ever turned out by a studio". In particular he praised the photography which he said "almost outdoes for sheer beauty the shots in *Street Angel* and *Sunrise*". Variety shared this opinion by proclaiming the film had "some of the most striking touches of composition seen on the screen since those swampland shots in *Sunrise*, which they often resemble." However the film was not a box office success as Fox Film Corporation did not promote the film.

DVD release

The film was released on DVD in North America by Fox on December 4, 2007. The film can be obtained three different ways:

- In the *Ford at Fox - The Collection* box set which is a 21 disc collection containing every film John Ford made at Fox.
- In the *Ford At Fox Collection: John Ford's Silent Epics* which also contains *Just Pals, Four Sons, The Iron Horse* and *3 Bad Men*.
- As a separate release also containing *3 Bad Men* on the opposite side of the disc.

The DVD begins with a disclaimer stating that the film has been brought to DVD using the best surviving elements possible. The DVD has an option to view the film accompanied with a musical score by Tim Curran.

Source (edited): "http://en.wikipedia.org/wiki/Hangman%27s_House"

Hearts of Oak (film)

Hearts of Oak is a 1924 drama film directed by John Ford. The film is considered to be lost.

Cast

- Hobart Bosworth - Terry Dunnivan
- Pauline Starke - Chrystal
- Theodore von Eltz - Ned Fairweather
- James Gordon - John Owen
- Francis Powers - Grandpa Dunnivan
- Jennie Lee - Grandma Dunnivan
- Francis Ford
- Frances Teague - Bridesmaid

Source (edited): "http://en.wikipedia.org/wiki/Hearts_of_Oak_(film)"

Hell Bent

Hell Bent is a 1918 Western film directed by John Ford and featuring Harry Carey. A print of the film exists in the Czechoslovak Film Archive.

Cast

- Harry Carey - Cheyenne Harry
- Duke R. Lee - Cimmaron Bill (as Duke Lee)
- Neva Gerber - Bess Thurston
- Vester Pegg - Jack Thurston
- Joe Harris - Beau Ross (as Joseph Harris)
- Steve Clemente - Undetermined Role
- Millard K. Wilson - Undetermined Role
- Molly Malone - Undetermined Role

Source (edited): "http://en.wikipedia.org/wiki/Hell_Bent"

Hitchin' Posts

Hitchin' Posts is a 1920 drama film directed by John Ford. The film is considered to be lost.

Cast

- Frank Mayo - Jefferson Todd
- Beatrice Burnham - Barbara Brereton
- C.E. Anderson - Captain of steamer
- Matthew Biddulph - Maj. Grey (as M. Biddulph)
- Mark Fenton - Col. Brereton
- Dagmar Godowsky - Octoroon
- Joe Harris
- Duke R. Lee - Col. Lancy (as Duke Lee)
- J. Farrell MacDonald - Joe Alabam (as J. Farrell McDonald)

Source (edited): "http://en.wikipedia.org/wiki/Hitchin%27_Posts"

Hoodman Blind

Hoodman Blind is a 1923 drama film directed by John Ford. The film is considered to be lost. It is a remake of a 1913 film of the same name directed by James Gordon.

Cast

- David Butler - Jack Yeulette
- Gladys Hulette - Nancy Yeulette / Jessie Walton
- Regina Connelly - Jessie Walton (the first)
- Frank Campeau - Mark Lezzard
- Marc McDermott - John Linden
- Trilby Clark - Mrs. John Linden
- Jack Walters - Bull Yeaman
- Eddie Gribbon - Battling Brown

Source (edited): "http://en.wikipedia.org/wiki/Hoodman_Blind"

How Green Was My Valley (film)

How Green Was My Valley is a 1941 drama film directed by John Ford. The film was produced by Darryl F. Zanuck, written by Philip Dunne, and based on the Richard Llewellyn novel of the same name. The film stars Walter Pidgeon, Maureen O'Hara, Anna Lee, Donald Crisp, and Roddy McDowall. It was nominated for ten Academy Awards, winning five and beating out such classics as *Citizen Kane*, *The Maltese Falcon*, *Suspicion* and *Sergeant York* for Best Picture.

The film tells the story of the Morgans, a close, hard-working Welsh family at the turn of the twentieth century in the South Wales coalfield at the heart of the South Wales Valleys. It chronicles a socio-economic way of life passing and the family unit disintegrating.

In 1990, *How Green Was My Valley* was selected for preservation in the United States National Film Registry by the Library of Congress as being "culturally, historically, or aesthetically significant".

Plot

The story is told through the eyes, and with the voice-over narration of Huw Morgan (Roddy McDowall), now a middle-aged man leaving his home, a mining town in the Rhondda Valley, and recalling the events that most impressed his younger self. The boy Huw is played by Roddy, but the voice-over is that of actor Irving Pichel, who is never seen in the film.

His first memories are of the marriage of his brother, Ivor (Patric Knowles), and the burgeoning, unspoken, and ill-fated romance of his sister, Angharad (Maureen O'Hara), with the new preacher, Mr. Gruffydd (Walter Pidgeon). Because of the forbidden nature of the romance, Angharad marries another man, whom she later divorces, and Mr. Gruffydd leaves the chapel in disgust after being subjected to untrue town gossip - his romance with Angharad is never consummated, nor do they ever marry. Still too young to work in the local coal mine like his father, Gwilym (Donald Crisp), and his five older brothers, Huw senses the seriousness of an imminent strike by the rift it creates between his father and the other boys when three of them move out of the family abode.

During the tensions of the strike, Huw saves his mother (Sara Allgood) from drowning and in so doing temporarily loses the use of his legs. As Gruffydd aids in Huw's recovery, insisting on a positive attitude, he suggests that it is only the first of many trials the boy will have to face. Other subplots are featured in the film. The film concludes with the death of the father in a mining accident.

Cast

Sara Allgood as Beth Morgan and Roddy McDowall as Huw Morgan.

- Walter Pidgeon as Mr. Gruffydd
- Maureen O'Hara as Angharad Morgan
- Anna Lee as Bronwyn, Ivor's wife
- Donald Crisp as Gwilym Morgan
- Roddy McDowall as Huw Morgan
- John Loder as Ianto Morgan
- Sara Allgood as Mrs. Beth Morgan
- Barry Fitzgerald as Cyfartha
- Patric Knowles as Ivor Morgan
- Morton Lowry as Mr. Jonas
- Arthur Shields as Mr. Parry
- Ann E. Todd as Ceinwen
- Frederick Worlock as Dr. Richards
- Richard Fraser as Davy Morgan
- Evan S. Evans as Gwilym Morgan
- James Monks as Owen Morgan
- Rhys Williams as Dai Bando
- Lionel Pape as Evans
- Ethel Griffies as Mrs. Nicholas
- Marten Lamont as Iestyn Evans

Background

William Wyler, the original director, saw the screen-test of McDowall and chose him for the part. Wyler was replaced later by director John Ford. Fox wanted to shoot the movie in Wales in Technicolor, but events in Europe during World War II made this impossible. Instead, Ford built a replica of the mining town at the nearly 3,000-acre (12 km) Fox Ranch in Malibu Canyon.

The cast had only one genuinely Welsh actor in a minor role, Rhys Williams.

Awards

Academy Award

- Best Picture - Darryl F. Zanuck (*won*)
- Best Director - John Ford (*won*)
- Best Supporting Actor - Donald Crisp (*won*)
- Best Black-and-White Cinematography - Arthur C. Miller (*won*)
- Best Black-and-White Art Direction-Interior Decoration - Richard Day, Nathan H. Juran and Thomas Little (*won*)
- Best Adapted Screenplay - Philip Dunne
- Best Supporting Actress - Sara Allgood
- Best Film Editing - James B. Clark
- Best Music, Scoring of a Dramatic Picture - Alfred Newman
- Best Recording Sound - Edmund H. Hansen

Other awards

- New York Film Critics Circle Awards: NYFCC Award; Best Director, John Ford; 1941.
- Argentine Film Critics Association Awards: Silver Condor; Best Foreign Film, John Ford, USA; 1943.
- 1990—National Film Registry.

Adaptations

How Green Was My Valley was adapted as a radio play on the March 22, 1942 broadcast of the Ford Theatre, with Sara Allgood, Donald Crisp, Roddy McDowell, Maureen O'Hara and Walter Pidgeon. It was also adapted on three broadcasts of Lux Radio Theater (September 21, 1942, March 31, 1947, and September 28, 1954) the first with Allgood, Crisp, O'Hara, McDowell and Pidgeon, the second with Crisp and David Niven, the third with Crisp and Donna Reed.

Source (edited): "http://en.wikipedia.org/wiki/How_Green_Was_My_Valley_(film)"

How the West Was Won (film)

How the West Was Won is a 1962 American epic Western film. The picture was one of the last "old-fashioned" epic films made by Metro-Goldwyn-Mayer to enjoy great success. It follows four generations of a family (starting as the Prescotts) as they move ever westward, from western New York state to the Pacific Ocean. Filmed in, and using pre-existing Cinerama curving widescreen process stock footage, the movie is set between 1839 and 1889.

The fundamental idea behind the film was to provide an episodic retelling of the progress of westward migration and development of America. It was inspired by a much longer and more complex series of historical narratives that appeared as a photo essay series, by the same name, three years earlier in *Life* magazine, which is acknowledged in the film's credits.

The all-star cast includes Carroll Baker, Walter Brennan, Lee J. Cobb, Andy Devine, Henry Fonda, Carolyn Jones, Karl Malden, Harry Morgan, Gregory Peck, George Peppard, Robert Preston, Debbie Reynolds, James Stewart, Eli Wallach, John Wayne, and Richard Widmark. The film is narrated by Spencer Tracy.

The movie consists of five segments, three directed by Henry Hathaway ("The Rivers", "The Plains" and "The Outlaws"), and one each by John Ford ("The Civil War") and George Marshall ("The Railroad"), with transitional sequences by the uncredited Richard Thorpe. The screenplay was written by John Gay (uncredited) and James R. Webb. Popular western author Louis L'Amour wrote a novelization of the screenplay.

In 1997, *How the West Was Won* was selected for preservation in the United States National Film Registry by the Library of Congress as being "culturally, historically, or aesthetically significant". The score was listed at #25 on AFI's *100 Years of Film Scores*.

Plot

The Rivers (1830s)

The settlers' raft is caught in rapids.

A family led by Zebulon Prescott (Karl Malden) sets out for the frontier west via the Erie Canal, the "west" at this time being the Illinois country. On the journey, they meet mountain man Linus Rawlings (James Stewart) who is traveling east to Pittsburgh to trade his furs. He and Zebulon's daughter Eve (Carroll Baker) are attracted to each other, but Linus is not ready to settle down.

Linus stops at an isolated trading post run by a murderous clan of river pirates headed by "Colonel" Hawkins (Walter Brennan). Linus is betrayed when he accompanies pretty Dora Hawkins (Brigid Bazlen) into a cave to see a "varmint". She stabs him in the back and pushes him into a deep hole. Fortunately, he is not seriously wounded, and is able to rescue the Prescott party from a similar fate. The bushwhacking thieves (Lee Van Cleef plays one), including Dora, are dispatched with rough frontier justice.

The settlers continue down the river, but their raft is caught in rapids and Zebulon and his wife Rebecca (Agnes Moorehead) drown. Linus, finding that he cannot live without Eve, reappears and marries her, even though she insists on homesteading at the spot where her parents died.

The Plains (1850s)

The wagon train is attacked by Cheyenne Indians.

Eve's sister Lily (Debbie Reynolds) chooses to go to St. Louis, where she finds work performing in a dance hall. She attracts the attention of professional gambler Cleve Van Valen (Gregory Peck). After overhearing that she has just inherited a California gold mine, and to avoid paying his debts to another gambler (John Larch), Cleve joins the wagon train taking her there. He and wagonmaster Roger Morgan (Robert Preston) court her along the way, but she turns them both down, much to the dismay of her new friend and fellow traveler Agatha Clegg (Thelma Ritter), who is searching for a husband.

Surviving an attack by Cheyenne Indians, Lily and Cleve arrive at the mine, only to find that it is now worthless. Cleve leaves. Lily returns to work in a dance hall in a literal "Camp Town," living out of a covered wagon. Morgan finds her and again proposes marriage in a rather unromantic way. She tells him, "No, not ever."

Later, Lily is singing in the music salon of a riverboat. By chance, Cleve is a passenger. When he hears Lily's voice, he leaves the poker table (and a winning hand) to propose to her, telling her of the opportunities waiting in the rapidly growing city of San Francisco. She accepts.

The Civil War (1861–1865)

American Civil War.

Linus joins the Union army as a captain in the American Civil War. Despite Eve's wishes, their son Zeb (George Peppard) eagerly enlists as well, looking for glory and an escape from farming. Corporal Peterson (Andy Devine) assures them the conflict won't last very long. The bloody Battle of Shiloh shows Zeb that war is nothing like he imagined and, unknown to him, his father Linus dies there. He encounters a similarly disillusioned Confederate (Russ Tamblyn) who suggests deserting, to which Zeb agrees.

However, by chance, they overhear a private conversation between Generals Ulysses S. Grant (Harry Morgan) and William Tecumseh Sherman (John Wayne). The rebel realizes he has the opportunity to rid the South of two of its greatest enemies and tries to shoot them, leaving Zeb no choice but to stab and kill him. Afterwards, Zeb rejoins the army.

When the war finally ends, he returns home, only to find his mother has died. She had lost the will to live after learning that Linus had been killed. Zeb gives his share of the family farm to his brother, who is more tied to the land, and leaves in search of a more interesting life.

The Railroad (1868)

The construction of railroad.

Following the daring riders from the Pony Express and the construction of the transcontinental telegraph line in the late 1860s, two ferociously competing railroad lines, the Central Pacific Railroad and the Union Pacific Railroad, one building west and the other east, open up new territory to eager settlers.

Zeb becomes a lieutenant in the U.S. cavalry, trying to maintain peace with the Indians with the help of grizzled buffalo hunter Jethro Stuart (Henry Fonda), an old friend of Linus. When ruthless railroad man Mike King (Richard Widmark) violates a treaty by building on Indian territory, the Arapaho Indians retaliate by stampeding buffalo through his camp, killing many, including women and children. Disgusted, Zeb resigns and heads to Arizona.

The Outlaws (1880s)

The desperadoes who want to rob the train.

In San Francisco, widowed Lily auctions off her possessions (she and Cleve had made and spent several fortunes) to pay her debts. She travels to Arizona, inviting Zeb and his family to oversee her remaining asset, a ranch.

Zeb (now a marshal), his wife Julie (Carolyn Jones) and their children meet Lily at Gold City's train station. However, Zeb also runs into an old enemy there, outlaw Charlie Gant (Eli Wallach). It is revealed that Zeb killed Gant's brother in a gunfight. When Gant makes veiled threats against Zeb and his family, Zeb turns to his friend and Gold City's marshal, Lou Ramsey (Lee J. Cobb), but Gant is not wanted for anything in that territory, so there is little Ramsey can do.

Zeb decides he has to act rather than wait for Gant to make good his threat to show up someday. Suspecting Gant of planning to rob an unusually large gold shipment being transported by train, he prepares an ambush with Ramsey's reluctant help. Gant and his entire gang (one member played by Harry Dean Stanton) are killed in the shootout. In the end, Lily and the Rawlingses travel to their new home.

A short epilogue shows Los Angeles and San Francisco in the early 1960s, including the famous four-level downtown freeway interchange and Golden Gate Bridge, indicating the growth of the West in 80 years.

Cast

- Carroll Baker as Eve Prescott Rawlings
- Lee J. Cobb as Marshal Lou Ramsey
- Henry Fonda as Jethro Stuart
- Carolyn Jones as Julie Rawlings
- Karl Malden as Zebulon Prescott
- Harry Morgan as Gen. Ulysses S. Grant
- Gregory Peck as Cleve Van Valen
- George Peppard as Zeb Rawlings
- Robert Preston as Roger Morgan
- Debbie Reynolds as Lilith 'Lily' Prescott
- James Stewart as Linus Rawlings
- Eli Wallach as Charlie Gant
- John Wayne as Gen. William Tecumseh Sherman
- Richard Widmark as Mike King
- Brigid Bazlen as Dora Hawkins
- Walter Brennan as Col. Jeb Hawkins
- David Brian as Lilith's attorney
- Andy Devine as Corporal Peterson
- Raymond Massey as President Abraham Lincoln
- Agnes Moorehead as Rebecca Prescott
- Thelma Ritter as Agatha Clegg
- Mickey Shaughnessy as Deputy Stover
- Russ Tamblyn as Confederate

deserter
- Spencer Tracy as Narrator

The film marked then sixty-six year old Raymond Massey's last appearance as Abraham Lincoln, a role that he had previously played on stage (*Abe Lincoln in Illinois* and the stage adaptation of *John Brown's Body*), on screen (*Abe Lincoln in Illinois*) and on television (*The Day Lincoln Was Shot*, and two more productions of *Abe Lincoln in Illinois*).

Lee Van Cleef, John Larch, Jay C. Flippen, Carleton Young and Harry Dean Stanton play very brief, uncredited roles.

Accolades

The film won three Academy Awards for:
- Best Writing, Story and Screenplay — Written Directly for the Screen (James R. Webb)
- Best Film Editing
- Best Sound

It was also nominated for:
- Best Picture
- Best Art Direction — Set Decoration, Color (George Davis, William Ferrari, Addison Hehr, Henry Grace, Don Greenwood, Jr., Jack Mills)
- Best Cinematography, Color
- Best Costume Design, Color
- Best Music, Score — Substantially Original (Alfred Newman and Ken Darby)

Production

How the West Was Won is one of only two dramatic feature films (the other being *The Wonderful World of the Brothers Grimm*) made using the three-strip Cinerama process. Although the picture quality when projected onto curved screens in theatres was stunning, attempts to convert the movie to a smaller screen suffer from that process's technical shortcomings. When seen in letterbox format the actors' faces are nearly indistinguishable in long shots.

John Ford complained about having to dress such huge sets since Cinerama photographed a much wider view than the standard single camera process to which Hollywood directors had become accustomed.

An even more difficult problem was that the film had to be shot with the actors artificially positioned out of dramatic and emotional frame, and out of synchronization with one another. Only when the three-print Cinerama process is projected upon a Cinerama screen will the positions and emotions of the actors synchronize, such as normal eye-contact or emotional harmony between actors in a dramatic sequence. In flat screen projection of the film, the actors appear to never make eye contact or relate to one another, so as to carry a complete scene to emotional or dramatic completion.

Stuntman Bob Morgan, husband of Yvonne De Carlo, was severely injured and lost a leg during an accident while filming.

The film would later inspire an ABC television series of the same name.

Restoration

"SmileBox" version of *How the West Was Won*, as seen on the Blu-ray release of 2008.

Crest Digital was given the task of restoring the original Cinerama negative for *How the West Was Won* in 2000 and built their own authentic Cinerama screening room in order to complete the process. There have also been efforts, led by HP, to combine the three image portions and make the Cinerama image look more acceptable on a flat screen. This has finally been accomplished on the latest DVD and Blu-ray Disc release. The lines at which the three Cinerama panels joined were formerly glaringly visible (as seen in the stills reproduced on this page), but this has been largely corrected on the Warner Bros. DVD and Blu-ray Disc, although the joins can still be seen in places, especially against bright backgrounds. The restoration also corrects some of the geometric distortions inherent in the process; for instance, in the final shot, the Golden Gate Bridge appears to curve in perspective as the camera flies underneath it, whereas in the Cinerama version, it breaks into three straight sections at different angles.

The Blu-ray also contains a "SmileBox" version, simulating the curved screen effect.

The aspect ratio of Cinerama was 2.59:1. Although Warner's new DVD release of the film states the Ultra Panavision 70 ratio of 2.89:1, which was used in selected shots.

The restored Warner Bros. release has been shown on television since October 2008, on the Encore Westerns channel.

Source (edited): "http://en.wikipedia.org/wiki/How_the_West_Was_Won_(film)"

Jackie (1921 film)

Jackie is a 1921 drama film directed by John Ford. The film is considered to be lost.

Cast

- Shirley Mason - Jackie
- William Scott - Mervyn Carter
- Harry Carter - Bill Bowman
- George Stone - Benny
- John Cook - Winter
- Elsie Bambrick - Millie

Source (edited): "http://en.wikipedia.org/wiki/Jackie_(1921_film)"

John Ford filmography

The following are the films directed by **John Ford**. He was credited as *Jack Ford* in all his silent films until *Cameo Kirby* in 1923. The Internet Movie Database lists Ford as directing 140 films from 1917 to 1966. Of Ford's silent films, only 15% of them are known to survive.

Documentaries about Ford
- *Directed by John Ford* (1971) directed by Peter Bogdanovich and narrated by Orson Welles
- *Directed by John Ford* (2006) restored longer version which premiered on Turner Classic Movies on 7 November 2006

Source (edited): "http://en.wikipedia.org/wiki/John_Ford_filmography"

Judge Priest

Judge Priest was released in 1934. The film was based on humorist Irvin S. Cobb's character Judge Priest. The film was directed by John Ford and produced by Sol M. Wurtzel in association with Fox Film. The film satirizes life in post-reconstruction Kentucky.

Cast
- Will Rogers as Judge William 'Billy' Priest
- Tom Brown as Jerome Priest
- Anita Louise as Ellie May Gillespie
- Henry B. Walthall as Reverend Ashby Brand
- David Landau as Bob Gillis
- Rochelle Hudson as Virginia Maydew
- Roger Imhof as Billy Gaynor
- Frank Melton as Flem Talley
- Charley Grapewin as Sergeant Jimmy Bagby
- Berton Churchill as Senator Horace Maydew
- Brenda Fowler as Mrs. Caroline Priest
- Francis Ford as Juror No. 12
- Hattie McDaniel as Aunt Dilsey
- Stepin Fetchit as Jeff Poindexter

Plot

In the year 1890, the honorable Judge William Priest enforces justice in an old Kentucky town. The film begins with the comedic trial of Jeff Poindexter. Jeff Poindexter, a black man, has been accused of stealing chickens. Although Judge Priest is presiding, he is reading a newspaper while Senator Horace Maydew argues the plaintiff's case. In fact, no one, but Senator Maydew, seems to care about the case. Jeff Poindexter sleeps through Senator Maydew's testimony. After Senator Maydew is finished with his argument, Judge Priest asks the sheriff to wake up Jeff Poindexter. When Jeff reveals he got his name from Major Randolph Poindexter, Judge Priest and the other confederate veterans in attendance become very excited. They praise Major Poindexter's ability to lick the Yankees. While the confederate veterans reminisce over the civil war, Senator Maydew complains that such history has nothing to do with the case. Judge Priest says it is relevant because Major Poindexter would often steal Yankee chickens. Next, Jeff reveals he was only trying to fish for catfish. Judge Priest, a fishing enthusiast himself, has a discussion with Jeff about his fishing. After the trial, Jeff lives with Judge Priest.

Judge Priest is sitting on his porch when his nephew, Rome, returns from a law school up north. Rome discovers his lover, Elli May, has found another man. Rome's mom, Caroline, is happy that Rome will not be intermingling with Elli May, a girl Caroline believes is not fit for a Priest. Caroline does not like Elli May because her mother is penniless and her father absent. Judge Priest, who desperately wants to see Elli May and Rome together, counters Caroline by saying that the Priest family has never stood for intolerance. That evening Elli May has her new lover, the Barber Flem Talley, over for lemonade. Flem Talley had been drinking before he arrived at Elli May's house. Elli May is not happy with Flem. Judge Priest, who had been observing Elli May and Flem from his porch next door, devises a plan to scare Flem away. After Elli May goes inside to prepare some lemonade, leaving Flem on the porch alone, Judge Priest hides behind a hedge and plays out a monologue. He pretends to be gossiping with another person about a gang of men with shotguns coming to get Flem Talley. In his monologue, the Judge confesses that he can do nothing until after the gang has committed murder, but then he will make sure the gang gets the justice they deserve. Of course, there was no gang, but the Judge successfully succeeds in scaring Flem. Flem gets in his buggy and leaves in a hurry. Judge Priest sends Rome, who was unaware of the Judge's actions to scare Flem, over to Elli May's house. Rome arrives on Elly May's porch just as Elly May comes out with the lemonade she had prepared.

That night Judge Priest goes out to sit next to his deceased wife's tombstone. She died in 1871, nineteen years before the film takes place. Nonetheless, Judge Priest shows no interest in remarrying. While Judge Priest sits next to his wife's tombstone he reveals that Senator Maydew has his eye on taking Judge Priest's spot on the bench. Judge Priest watches, unobserved, as Bob Gillus places flowers next to Elli May's mother's tombstone. Judge Priest is confused, but he does not contemplate it further.

The next morning Judge Priest goes into town. Confederate veteran Jimmy tells Judge Priest he is cleaning his gun because one never knows what the Yankees are going to do. When Judge Priest talks to Bob Gillus about getting new horseshoes, Judge Priest notices Bob has a bullet scar on his arm. When Judge Priest brings up the bullet scar, Bob refuses to elaborate beyond receiving it up north after the civil war.

Judge Priest leaves town to go catfish fishing with Jeff. Judge Priest asks Jeff to prepare the beef liver bait. Upon finding no more beef liver bait, Jeff explains, "Looks like that liver done walk off by itself."

Judge Priest, just slightly irritated, sends Jeff to get more bait. Jeff throws his shoes over his shoulder and walks toward town. Judge Priest asks him why he does not put on his shoes. Jeff replies, "I'm saving them for when my feet wear out." "As much sitting around as you do it won't be your feet that wear out," responds Judge Priest.

Jeff and Judge Priest return home to prepare for the Church Ice Cream Festival and Candy Pull. Judge Priest tells Jeff he is not allowed to wear his nice raccoon coat. Jeff says it is rabbit fur. Judge Priest explains to Jeff that it is raccoon fur because he took it from a rich Yankee. At the Church the Black women are busy preparing the taffy. The Black women happily sing songs about Jesus as they work. Judge Priest runs into Reverend Brand upon entering the churchyard. Reverend Brand scolds Judge Priest for not coming to church enough. Although Senator Maydew attends church every Sunday, Reverend Brand clearly favors Judge Priest for the judge's bench. Judge Priest confesses to Reverend Brand he does not have the grammar or rhetoric that Senator Maydew possesses. Meanwhile, Senator Maydew tells church members that he will not make the race about personalities. Of course, by stating this, Senator Maydew is making it clear he believes Judge Priest's personality is not fit for the job of judge.

When the candy pull begins, Rome's mom, Caroline, pairs Rome with Virginia Maydew. Virginia is the Senator's daughter. Caroline feels that Virginia is well suited for Rome because she is from an affluent family. Rome, on the other hand, would rather be paired with Elli May. Judge Priest rescues Rome. Judge Priest tells Rome and Virginia he will take Rome's place while he gets more butter. Rome, realizing his Uncle has come to relieve him, leaves the Candy Pull with Elli May.

Later in the week, Judge Priest goes to get a haircut from barber Flem Talley. While the Judge is receiving his haircut, Elli May strolls by. Flem whistles loudly at her. Bob Gillus, who had been waiting for his haircut, stands up and punches Flem in the face. Judge Priest applauds Bob Gillus for his behavior.

Flem and his friends plan their revenge. They hide in the billiard room of the local bar. They plan on ambushing Bob Gillus with their pool cues. When Bob Gillus gets ambushed he pulls a knife on Flem and fleas the scene. Bob hires Rome to defend him in court. Rome is ecstatic because Bob is his first client. Caroline, on the other hand, is not happy that her son is defending an outcast northerner over a fight with a girl. Elli May, the girl who Bob stood up for, tells Caroline that she knows Caroline does not believe she is good enough for her son. "However," Elli May says, "If Rome were half as mean as you, Rome would not be good enough for me."

In court, Senator Maydew, who represents Flem, asks Judge Priest to step down from the bench because of his nephew's participation in the case as well as the Judge's direct involvement at the barbershop. Judge Priest obliges and appoints the honorable Floyd Bailey to serve as Judge. On the first day of testimony Rome is unable to convince the jury that Bob is innocent. The jury consists of Confederate veterans who show no sympathy for someone from up north. After one day of deliberation all that remains is closing arguments.

That evening, Reverend Brand tells Judge Priest that Bob Gillus is Elli May's father. Judge Priest realizes that this changes the whole nature of the case. In order to reopen the case, Judge Priest offers his raccoon coat to Jeff for delivering a letter of evidence to Senator Maydew. Judge Priest asks Jeff to play his drums outside the courtroom to dramatize Reverend Brand's testimony. Jeff says he can play the popular Union song Marching Through Georgia. Judge Priest tells Jeff, "I got you outta one lynching, if I catch you playing Marching Through Georgia I'll join the lynchers."

The next morning Judge Priest and Rome represent Bob Gillus together. They bring Reverend Brand up to the witness stand. Reverend Brand tells the jury that he served as a captain of artillery for the Southern Confederacy. Reverend Brand recounts how, in desperation for more soldiers, he took men off the chain gang. One of these men was Bob Gillus. Reverend Brand explains, to the pleasure of the jury of Confederate veterans, how brave Bob was as he fought for the confederates. While Reverend Brand recounts stories of Bob running through Union lines, Jeff and his black friends play celebratory music outside an open courthouse window. Finally, Reverend Brand reveals that he knew Bob Gillus 25 years ago as Roger Gillespiere. Bob Gillus, Reverend Brand tells the jury, is Elli May Gillespiere's father. Elli Mae, who was in attendance, is shocked to hear this. The jury began celebrating their war hero, Bob Gillus. Later that day, the town held its annual veteran's parade. Bob Gillus had the honor of leading the parade.

Stepin Fetchit

Stepin Fetchit's character in Judge Priest, Jeff Poindexter, is the early twentieth-century stereotypical black man. Jeff Poindexter is extremely dull, slow and lazy. Stepin Fetchit (actually born Lincoln Perry) built his reputation by stereotyping blacks in this manner. It was this portrayal of blacks that enraged many black activists who were fighting the very stereotypes he was portraying. Many blacks labeled him a traitor and purposely avoided events that he was scheduled to attend.

Stepin Fetchit was born in 1902, in Key West, Florida. Although he was uneducated, he was a very shrewd and calculating man. Despite the on screen appearance of being dim-witted, Stephin Fetchit was aggressive with the moguls and producers who controlled Hollywood. Fetchit had pride in being a "militant Negro". Fetchit was able to work with both black and whites, allowing him to reach high levels of success. In this way Fetchit was the first Black actor to fight for equal treatment from Hollywood executives.

In his role as Jeff Poindexter, Director John Ford gave Fetchit some room to expand his comic performance. When Judge Priest asked Jeff why he was not wearing his shoes, Jeff comically replied, "I'm saving them for when my feet wear out."

Stepin Fetchit was known for attending lavish parties and causing mischief while off the studio lot. In fact, Fox Studios would hire a white bodyguard to ensure that he did not get into trouble while he was off set. Right before the shooting of Judge Priest, Fetchit caused a commotion at a benefit show at the Apollo Theater in New York City. When he arrived back in Hollywood for the filming of Judge Priest, Fetchit's behavior was much better. In fact, only once was Fetchit late for a shoot (he forgot his make-up kit).

Haitte McDaniel

Hattie McDaniel played Aunt Dilsey in Judge Priest. Hattie McDaniel was just beginning her trek to stardom when she shot Judge Priest. Before starring in Judge Priest she was a relatively unknown actress. Stepin Fetchit apparently doubted her acting abilities at the beginning of shooting Judge Priest, but soon realized he was working with a very talented black performer. Director John Ford noted McDaniel's acting talents. Ford cut some of Fetchit's scenes and gave McDaniel additional scenes. This created an initial rift between these two pioneering black actors. Hattie McDaniel would eventually surpass Stephen Fetchit in fame.

Like Stepin Fetchit, Hattie McDaniel plays into Black stereotypes characteristic of the early twentieth century. She works in the kitchen as a maid. However, she loves to smile and sing while she works. She sings the song "Massa Jesus Wrote Me a Note" while making taffy at the church candy pull.

Will Rogers

Superstar Will Rogers played Judge Priest. The film played a major role in earning Will Rogers the number one box office star of 1934. Will Rogers earned lots of critical praise for his role in Judge Priest. Many critics attend that Will Rogers simply fell right into the role with his heart-warming personality. Rogers managed a balance of comedic one-liners with serious dramatics. The Tulsa Daily World summed up Roger's performance: "The star's portrayal of Judge Priest has the mark of authenticity upon it…the unique blending of unique talent with a rich and splendid role."

Judge Priest is an eccentric judge. Although his wife dies 19 years before the film takes place, he shows no interest in remarrying. He sometimes stumbles his words, but he shows his wit throughout the film. The Judge, despite all his talk of being a confederate veteran, finds his best friend to be the black Jeff Poindexter. Judge Priest has pride in his tolerance for others.

Will Rogers passed away in a tragic plane crash on August 15, 1935, just a year after the release of Judge Priest. His death came as shock to people across the globe.

Connection To Birth of a Nation

Henry B. Walthall plays the role of Reverend Ashby Brand in Judge Priest. Twenty years before Judge Priest was released, Walthall starred as the Little Colonel in D. W. Griffith's *The Birth of a Nation*. In Judge Priest Reverend Brand recounts fighting in the civil war with Bob Gillus. Reverend Brand and Bob Gillus both fought for the Confederate Army in the Civil War. As Reverend Brand explains to the jury the courage displayed by Bob Gillus, scenes from the civil war play in the film. Reverend Brand's face is faintly crossed with battle scenes. The civil war battle scenes displayed in the background resemble similar battle scenes in *The Birth of a Nation*. In both cases the war was being displayed from a Confederate perspective. The reason John Ford plays tribute to Birth of a Nation is not known.

Portraying Post-Reconstruction South

In Judge Priest John Ford pokes fun at the Southern United States, post the reconstruction era. By setting the film in Kentucky, 1890, the film is able to critique the south. Judge Priest portrays the town as being unable to let go of the past. Many of the male citizens of the town, including Judge Priest himself, were Civil War veterans. All the veterans fought for the Confederates. The town's citizens refer to Yankees several times. Every time Yankee is mentioned, an aura of disgust and hatred comes over the character. One town citizen cleans his gun because, as he explains it, "You never know what them Yankees are going to do."

At the end of the film the town happily participates in their annual Confederate Veteran's Parade; complete with Confederate flags, not American flags, strewn throughout the parade. When Bob Gillus was on trial the jury was ready to convict him when they believed he was an outsider from the north. When the jury discovers that he was a Confederate War hero they release him on all charges. During Jeff Poindexter's trial, Judge Priest shows he would rather reminisce with his fellow Confederate War Veterans about the Civil War than proceed with the arguments in the trial. Even the town Reverend, a man of God, fought for the Confederate's in the civil war.

Judge Priest shows a South that does not have a lot going on besides talk of the Confederate past. The entire town, it seems, is in attendance at the trial concerning a small brawl between a barber and handyman. The entire town attends the Church Ice Cream Social and Candy Pull. The statement that Judge Priest and Director John Ford make is that the reason the South is unable to move past the Confederacy is they are too bored.

A Stereotypical Portrayal African-Americans

Judge Priest portrays its Black roles controversially. Time Magazine deemed Judge Priest one of the twenty-five "Most Important Films on Race." Most of this controversy stems from Stepin Fetchit's stereotypical black portrayal of Jeff Poindexter. In addition, Hattie McDaniel portrays Aunt Dilsey as a stereotypical, happy, black houseservant. In Judge Priest, Blacks are portrayed as happily submissive to the whites. For example, when Rome comes running home, Jeff Poindexter throws open the gate for him. While the whites are all having a good time celebrating at the church social, all the black townspeople are busily working preparing the candy. The blacks happily prepare the taffy. This does not play into the stereotypical "lazy" black worker. Rather, this is how many southern slave owners viewed their slaves: happy to labor for the white man. John Ford satirizes the slave owner's moral justification for slavery.

The film, despite taking place in the South, shows Blacks and whites getting along very well. In fact, Judge Priest and Jeff Poindexter (a black man) are almost best friends in the film. It is an awkward friendship. They go fishing together. However, when Jeff forgets the bait he is forced to go back to town. Jeff Poindexter, on the other hand, does not join the Judge when he plays the elitist sport, Croquet, with his white friends. Stepin Fetchit said this about his on screen relationship with superstar Will Rogers: "When people saw me and Will Rogers like brothers, that said something to them."

The only character that shows any animosity to black people is Judge Priest's antagonist, Senator Maydew. Senator Maydew, when arguing for the conviction of Jeff Poindexter, says Jeff is a "confirmed Chicken thief" who has "no place in this God-fearing community."

There are several racial contradictions that play out in Judge Priest. For instance, although Judge Priest symbolizes the tolerant southerner he has one of the most racially horrific lines in film. When Jeff asks the Judge if he can play the popular Union song Marching Through Georgia, Judge Priest tells Jeff, "I got you outta one lynching, if I catch you playing Marching Through Georgia I'll join the lynchers." This line makes light of a very serious subject. Lynching was very much alive in the 1930s when Judge Priest was produced.

The blacks in Judge Priest celebrated the Confederacy with the whites. The blacks happily joined with the whites during the Confederate Veterans parade. Additionally, when Reverend Brand recounts his glory days with the Confederate Army, it was the black male populace outside creating the epic music to emotionalize Reverend Brand's story. The blacks celebrate the proslavery Confederates right alongside the whites.

Soundtrack

- Hattie McDaniel, Melba Brown, Thelma Brown, Vera Brown, Will Rogers and others - "My Old Kentucky Home, Good Night" (Music and lyrics by Stephen Foster)
- Hattie McDaniel - "Aunt Dilsey's Improvisation" (Written by Hattie McDaniel)
- "Love's Old Sweet Song (Just a Song at Twilight)" (Music by J.L. Molloy, lyrics by J. Clifton Bingham)
- Hattie McDaniel and others at the festival - "Massa Jesus Wrote Me a Note" (Music by Cyril J. Mockridge, lyrics by Dudley Nichols and Lamar Trotti)
- "Old Folks at Home (Swanee River)" (Written by Stephen Foster)
- "Old Black Joe" (Written by Stephen Foster)
- "(I Wish I Was in) Dixie's Land" (Written by Daniel Decatur Emmett)
- Hattie McDaniel - "The Little Brown Jug" (Music and lyrics by Joseph Winner)
- Hattie McDaniel - "Aunt Dilsey's Song" (Music by Cyril J. Mockridge, lyrics by Dudley Nichols and Lamar Trotti)

Source (edited): "http://en.wikipedia.org/wiki/Judge_Priest"

Just Pals

Just Pals is a 1920 Western film directed by John Ford. It was Ford's first film for the Fox Film Corporation.

Cast

- Buck Jones - Bim
- Helen Ferguson - Mary Bruce
- George Stone - Bill
- Duke R. Lee - Sheriff
- William Buckley - Harvey Cahill
- Eunice Murdock Moore - Mrs. Stone
- Bert Appling - Brakeman
- Edwin B. Tilton - Dr. Stone (as Edwin Booth Tilton)
- Slim Padgett - Outlaw
- John B. Cooke - Constable
- Pedro León - Undetermined Role
- Ida Tenbrook

Source (edited): "http://en.wikipedia.org/wiki/Just_Pals"

Kentucky Pride

Kentucky Pride is a 1925 drama film directed by John Ford. A print of the film exists at the Museum of Modern Art film archive.

Cast

- Gertrude Astor - Mrs. Beaumont
- Peaches Jackson - Virginia Beaumont
- J. Farrell MacDonald - Donovan
- Man o' War
- Winston Miller - Danny Donovan

- Belle Stoddard - Mrs. Donovan
- Malcolm Waite - Carter
- Henry B. Walthall - Mr. Beaumont

Source (edited): "http://en.wikipedia.org/wiki/Kentucky_Pride"

Lightnin'

Lightnin' is a 1925 comedy film directed by John Ford. It was based on a successful play that played 1,291 performances starting in 1918 at the Gaiety Theatre (New York). It was remade by Henry King for Fox in 1930 as an early talkie starring Will Rogers with support from Louise Dresser and Joel McCrea.

Cast
- Jay Hunt - William 'Lightnin' Bill' Jones
- Wallace MacDonald - John Marvin
- Richard Travers - Mr. Raymond Thomas
- J. Farrell MacDonald - Judge Lemuel Townsend
- Otis Harlan - Zeb
- Edythe Chapman - Mrs. Bill Jones
- Madge Bellamy - Miss Millie Jones
- Ethel Clayton - Margaret Davis
- Brandon Hurst - Everett Hammond
- James A. Marcus - Sheriff Blodgett (as James Marcus)
- Erville Alderson - Courtroom Attendant (uncredited)
- Nora Cecil - Passerby in Buggy (uncredited)
- Tommy Hicks - Otis Harlan's Son (uncredited)
- Peter Mazutis - Oscar (uncredited)
- Ida Moore - Courtroom Observer (uncredited)

Source (edited): "http://en.wikipedia.org/wiki/Lightnin%27"

Little Miss Smiles

Little Miss Smiles is a 1922 drama film directed by John Ford. The film is considered to be lost.

Cast
- Shirley Mason - Esther Aaronson
- Gaston Glass - Dr. Jack Washton
- George B. Williams - Papa Aaronson (as George Williams)
- Martha Franklin - Mama Aaronson
- Arthur Rankin - Davie Aaronson
- Alfred Testa - Louis Aaronson
- Richard Lapan - Leon Aaronson
- Sidney D'Albrook - 'The Spider'
- Baby Blumfield - Baby Aaronson

Source (edited): "http://en.wikipedia.org/wiki/Little_Miss_Smiles"

Marked Men (1919 film)

Marked Men (1919) is a Western film directed by John Ford and starring Harry Carey. It is a remake of the 1916 film *The Three Godfathers*, which also starred Carey. The film is considered to be a lost film.

Cast
- Harry Carey - Cheyenne Harry
- Joe Harris
- Ted Brooks
- Charles Le Moyne
- J. Farrell MacDonald
- Winifred Westover
- David Kirby - (uncredited)

Source (edited): "http://en.wikipedia.org/wiki/Marked_Men_(1919_film)"

Mary of Scotland (film)

Mary of Scotland is a 1936 RKO film starring Katharine Hepburn as the 16th century ruler, Mary, Queen of Scots. Directed by John Ford, it is an adaptation of the 1933 Maxwell Anderson play by Dudley Nichols. The play starred Helen Hayes as Mary. It is largely in blank verse.

Accuracy

The film does not keep close to the historical truth, portraying Mary as something of a wronged martyr and her husband, James Hepburn, Earl of Bothwell (played by Fredric March), as a romantic hero (the character is always called "Bothwell" in the film because the real figure was an ancestor of Hepburn and the studio was worried about appearances).

Cast
- Katharine Hepburn as Mary Stuart
- Fredric March as Bothwell
- Florence Eldridge as Elizabeth Tudor
- Douglas Walton as Darnley
- John Carradine as Rizzio
- Robert Barrat as Morton
- Gavin Muir as Leicester
- Ian Keith as Moray
- Moroni Olsen as John Knox. Olsen was the only member of the film's cast to repeat his original stage role.
- William Stack as Ruthven
- Ralph Forbes as Randolph
- Alan Mowbray as Throckmorton
- Frieda Inescort as Mary Beaton
- Donald Crisp as Huntly
- David Torrence as Lindsay
- Molly Lamont as Mary Livingstone
- Anita Colby as Mary Fleming

- Jean Fenwick as Mary Seton
- Lionel Pape as Burghley
- Alec Craig as Donal
- Mary Gordon as Nurse
- Monte Blue as Messenger
- Leonard Mudie as Maitland
- Brandon Hurst as Airan
- Wilfred Lucas as Lexington
- D'Arcy Corrigan as Kirkcaldy
- Frank Baker as Douglas
- Cyril McLaglen as Faudoncide
- Doris Lloyd as Fisherman's Wife
- Robert Warwick as Sir Francis Knollys

Reception

The film is highly regarded by some critics today, but in its time was a box office flop. It was one of the films that led to Katharine Hepburn's being labeled "box office poison" in the late 1930s, leading to her move to MGM and her great comeback in *The Philadelphia Story*.

Source (edited): "http://en.wikipedia.org/wiki/Mary_of_Scotland_(film)"

Men Without Women (film)

Men Without Women (1930) is an American drama film directed and written by John Ford, from the script by James Kevin McGuinness. The film also starred Kenneth MacKenna, Frank Albertson, and J. Farrell MacDonald.

Plot

Aboard the U.S. submarine S13 in the China seas, Chief Torpedoman Burke goes about his duties. In reality, he is Quartermaine, the infamous former commander of the British ship Royal Scot, which was sunk by Germans with a Field Marshal aboard. Quartermaine had told his sweetheart that the Field Marshal would be aboard, not knowing that she was an informant for the enemy. When the S13 sinks, Burke takes charge when the commander, Ensign Price, is unable to command. Burke must keep his mates alive long enough on the bottom of the sea for rescuers to arrive.

The film opens in Shanghai with a shore party of rowdy American sailors going partying an enormous establishment surrounded by women in the world's largest bar.

Cast

- Kenneth MacKenna as Chief Torpedoman Burke
- Frank Albertson as Ensign Albert Edward Price
- J. Farrell MacDonald as Costello
- Warren Hymer as Kaufman
- Paul Page as Handsome
- Walter McGrail as Joe Cobb
- Stuart Erwin as Radioman Jenkins
- George LeGuere as Curly Pollock
- Charles K. Gerrard as Commander Weymouth
- Ben Hendricks Jr. as Murphy
- Harry Tenbrook as Dutch Winkler
- Warner Richmond as Lieutenant Commander Briddwell

Release

The film premiered on January 31, 1930, in New York City. It was filmed on Santa Catalina Island, California, and was released by the Fox Film Corporation.

Source (edited): "http://en.wikipedia.org/wiki/Men_Without_Women_(film)"

Mister Roberts (1955 film)

Mister Roberts is a 1955 CinemaScope comedy-drama film directed by John Ford and Mervyn LeRoy, and starring Henry Fonda as Mister Roberts. Based on the 1946 novel and 1948 Broadway play, the film was nominated for Best Picture and Best Sound, Recording Oscars; Jack Lemmon received the Academy Award for Best Supporting Actor.

Synopsis

The film takes place on an American Naval cargo ship the, USS *Reluctant*, during the waning days of World War II. The ship's captain, Morton (James Cagney), is proud of his spotless record supplying the U.S. fleet. His command style is heavy-handed: he refuses to let the crew remove their shirts during hot days working in the cargo hold and has not granted his men "liberty" for at least two years, despite frequent requests by his executive officer, Lieutenant Douglas Roberts (Henry Fonda). Roberts has an excellent relationship with the crew, often bending the rules to allow them some leeway. For Morton's reputation for timely handling of cargo, an impressed admiral gave him a palm tree, which he cherishes and keeps in a dirt-filled bucket near the ship's bridge. However, the crew despises the tree and the captain himself and it is widely known by the crew that Roberts, not Morton, is primarily responsible for the ship's efficiency.

The captain holds the naval rank of Lieutenant Commander. Morton shows Roberts in the ship's safe, a Commander's hat with the scrambled eggs (gold braids) on the visor. Morton feels that if the ship continues to set cargo records the admiral will give Morton a promotion to Commander.

Roberts, despite his positive outlook, has grown tired of his dull duties and has repeatedly requested transfer to a unit on the front lines of the Pacific theatre. Morton has turned down every request. The captain realizes the ship's reputation for success is due to Roberts and not himself. He determines to keep Roberts on board by fair means or foul. Morton reveals later on that he endured a tough childhood as a busboy, constantly bullied by those of higher social status, during his time on passenger ships in the Merchant Marine, especially people who were college-educated like Roberts and thus has a deep personal hatred of "college boys". Roberts left medical school to enter the Navy.

Roberts bypasses the chain of command to request crew liberty from one of Morton's superiors. Liberty is granted and the ship sails to a South Pacific island, but Morton denies the crew their small vacation. After a heated conversation with Roberts, Morton grants the crew their liberty on the conditions that Roberts not request transfer ever again and that he will deal much more firmly with the crew. Roberts reluctantly acquiesces for the sake of the crew's liberty.

On the island, the ship's crew acts deplorably: they quickly get drunk, start fights, violently crash a party at the local embassy and are often hauled back to the ship by the Army's military police. One sailor steals a motorcycle and the ship's secretary, Dolan (Ken Curtis), steals a Navy Goat belonging to Admiral Wentworth, USN. Eventually, a large unit of the Navy's shore patrol arrives and surrounds the ship, preventing any of the crew from going ashore. The next morning, Morton returns to the ship from a dressing-down by the port admiral. Morton boards the ship yelling about having been told to leave port immediately.

The men of the ship are mystified by Roberts' new strict attitude. Morton falsely hints to them that Roberts is interested in a promotion. When a crew member informs Roberts of a new Navy policy which might assist him in getting a transfer despite the captain's opposition, Roberts responds sharply and refuses to take advantage of it. Roberts' friendly rapport with the crew is affected.

News of the Allied victory in Europe arrives and Roberts becomes further depressed, knowing the war may end soon without him seeing any combat. His mood breaks soon after, having been inspired by a radio speech. He takes the captain's palm tree and throws it overboard. Morton, unable to determine who did it, orders the crew to battle stations. He eventually realizes that Roberts is the only person who would have the nerve. He summons Roberts to his quarters and begins accusing him, but is so angry that he becomes ill. Because a microphone has been left open during the confrontation, the crew overhears the conversation and learns the truth.

Several weeks later, Roberts receives a transfer, even though he had kept his bargain with the captain and not requested one. The ship's doctor confides to Roberts that the crew had risked court-martial by submitting a forged transfer request. Before Roberts leaves, the crew made him a medal, Order of the Palm, for "action against the enemy".

Several weeks later, Ensign Pulver (Jack Lemmon), a lazy, self-serving, and meek junior officer who shared a cabin with Roberts and has taken his place as cargo chief, receives a pair of letters. One is from Roberts himself who speaks enthusiastically about his new assignment on the front lines near Okinawa, and respect for the men on the *Reluctant* for refusing to surrender to a force as deadly as combat: boredom. He goes on saying that he is looking at the medal and would rather have it than the Medal of Honor. The second letter, from "Forenel" a friend of Pulver's on the destroyer, USS *Livingston*, the same ship as Mr. Roberts, informs him that Roberts was killed in combat. "A Japanese kamikaze hits a 40mm battery and goes through into the wardroom, Doug was getting a cup of coffee." A furious and emboldened Pulver throws the captain's second palm tree overboard and marches into Morton's cabin, angrily demanding to know why Morton has canceled the showing of a film that night. Morton realizes things will be just as tough with Pulver as they were with Roberts.

Background

Fonda was not the original choice to star in the film version; Warner Bros. was considering William Holden or Marlon Brando for the lead role. The studio thought Fonda had been on stage and off the screen so long (8 years) that he was no longer a movie box office draw. In addition, when filming began he was 49, much older than the average lieutenant junior grade. Fonda was only hired because director John Ford insisted on it;

Also featured were James Cagney as Captain Morton, William Powell (in his last feature film) as "Doc", Jack Lemmon as Ensign Pulver (for which he won his first Academy Award, Best Supporting Actor), Betsy Palmer, Ward Bond, Philip Carey, Nick Adams, Ken Curtis, Harry Carey, Jr. and Martin Milner. The screenplay was written by Joshua Logan and Frank S. Nugent.

The movie was directed by John Ford, Mervyn LeRoy and Joshua Logan (uncredited). While directing the film, Ford had personality conflicts with actors Henry Fonda and James Cagney. When Ford met Cagney at the airport, the director warned that they would "tangle asses," which caught Cagney by surprise. Cagney later said: "I would have kicked his brains out. He was so goddamned mean to everybody. He was truly a nasty old man." The next day, Cagney was slightly late on set, and Ford became incensed. Cagney cut short the imminent tirade, saying: "When I started this picture, you said that we would tangle asses before this was over. I'm ready now – are you?" Ford backed down and walked away and he and Cagney had no further conflicts on the set.

Nevertheless, Ford was replaced by LeRoy after difficulties with Fonda (Ford apparently punched Fonda in the jaw during a heated argument), and a gall bladder attack that necessitated emergency surgery. It has been widely speculated which scenes were directed by LeRoy. Jack Lemmon shed some light on this issue in his DVD commentary: "Mervyn LeRoy would watch all of the rushes that Ford had shot prior to his temporary departure and decided to shoot them the way John Ford would have shot 'em."

The DVD release of this film includes an audio commentary of Jack Lemmon years before he died. In the commentary, he recounts some stories of his experience making the film and his views on acting. During the production of the film, Jack Lemmon started a long-time friendship with Cagney which lasted until Cagney's death in 1986. Prior to his appearance in his first film, years before *Mister Roberts*, he started in live television. In one particular performance, Lemmon decided to play his character differently. He decided to play the character left-handed, which is opposite to his own way of movement. With much practice, he pulled off the performance without anyone noticing the change. This change even fooled Lemmon's wife at the time. A few years went by and Jack met Cagney on their way to Midway Island to film *Mister Roberts*. They introduced themselves, and Cagney chimed in, "Are you still fooling people into believing you're left handed?" They had a great laugh and a strong friendship was born. As Lemmon noted, this was an example of Cagney's ability to observe human behavior for his acting.

Henry Fonda wrote in his 1982 autobiography, *My Life*, that he believed that as good as the movie is, the play is even better. The film was William Powell's last movie, although he died decades later in 1984. It was also James Cagney's last movie for Warner Brothers, the studio that had propelled him to stardom 25 years before and the studio to which he had spent the majority of his career under contract.

The Navy vessel which played the role of USS *Reluctant* ("the Bucket") in the movie's exterior shots was the USNS *New Bedford* (AKL-17) used for filming while she was at Midway Island in August 1954 and later off Kaneohe Bay, Oahu, Hawaii between 30 September and 7 October. All but one of the Navy's AKLs were built as U.S. Army FS type cargo vessels, some of which were transferred to the Navy after WWII ended. As it was, an AKL carried a much smaller crew than the USS *Virgo* (AKA-20) which Thomas Heggen served on during the war. In the movie, Mr. Roberts says to Doc that there are "65 men" aboard which would have been far too many for an AKL. The "palm tree" was located on a "deck" built for the movie by extending the small deckhouse of the AKL and building movie set ladders to the bridge and main deck. The crew, when going below to their berthing compartment, are shown in the movie to be descending into the cargo hold.

Television and sequels

The film was the basis of a 1965 television series of the same name, and was remade for television in 1984 as a live telecast.

Mister Roberts was followed by a film sequel, *Ensign Pulver* (1964), with Robert Walker, Jr. taking over the Lemmon role. It also starred Burl Ives as Captain Morton, Walter Matthau, Larry Hagman, and Jack Nicholson. Much of the screenplay was derived from Heggen's original book.

Source (edited): "http://en.wikipedia.org/wiki/Mister_Roberts_(1955_film)"

Mogambo

Mogambo is a 1953 film directed by John Ford, featuring Clark Gable, Ava Gardner, Grace Kelly and Donald Sinden. The film was adapted by John Lee Mahin from the play by Wilson Collison.

Kelly won a Golden Globe for Best Supporting Actress (1954), and the film was nominated for two Oscars, Best Actress in a Leading Role (Gardner), and Best Actress in a Supporting Role (Kelly). The film was also nominated for a BAFTA Film Award (Best Film from any Source USA).

Mogambo is a lavish remake of the classic film *Red Dust* (1932). The earlier movie also featured Gable in the lead role.

Eloise Y. 'Honey Bear' Kelly (Gardner) arrives at a remote African outpost, looking for a rich maharajah acquaintance, only to find he has decided to cancel his trip. While waiting for the next river boat out, she toys with hardworking big game hunter Victor Marswell (Gable), who (initially) has no respect for her type. When the river boat returns it brings with it Donald Nordley (Sinden) and his wife Linda (Grace Kelly) ready to go on safari. Miss Kelly departs. Later that day Mr. Nordley is taken ill with a reaction to his tsetse fly inoculations. From this it transpires the Nordleys wish to make the longer and more arduous trip to record gorillas. Marswell declines to take them. Later that night Miss Kelly returns in a row boat after the river steamer has run aground farther down river. There is some friction between Miss Kelly and Mrs. Nordley while her husband recovers after Miss Kelly witnesses Mrs. Nordley and Marswell together.

After Donald Nordley has recovered, Marswell agrees to go up into the gorilla country, taking Miss Kelly halfway to join the District Commissioner and travel back by that route. However, when they get there, they find the commissioner badly wounded by only recently belligerent natives. With a column of reinforcements days away, the small party is able to narrowly escape, taking the mortally wounded commissioner with them. Miss Kelly is thus forced to continue with the Nordleys and Marswell.

Meanwhile, a serious romance is developing between Marswell and Mrs. Nordley, and everyone in the party is aware except Mr. Nordley. The situation has become so tense that it is leading to clashes between Mr. Nordley and other members of the group. Miss Kelly tries to warn Mrs. Nordley of Marswell's character but is rebuffed. Marswell himself, while setting up to photograph and capture gorillas with Nordley, even attempts to tell Nordley, but then a charging "bull" gorilla appears and he is forced to shoot the beast, cutting off his confession.

Having killed the leader of the gorilla troop, Marswell becomes depressed and that night in camp begins a bout of heavy drinking in his tent. It is then that Miss Kelly shows up and throws herself across his lap and requests a drink for herself. She and Marswell are drowning their sorrows and lauding each other as friends, and their drinking leads to some light-hearted kissing and caressing, at which point Mrs. Nordley appears. Marswell's dismissive remarks on her infatuation with him as "the White Hunter" enrages her, and she takes Marswell's pistol and shoots him as he tries to flee the tent, wounding him in his right arm. When the rest of the camp shows up, Miss Kelly explains that Marswell has been making advances at Mrs. Nordley for some time, and now having done so in a drunken state, has forced her to shoot him as a last resort. Everyone laughs and goes off, with Mr. Nordley saying that Marswell is lucky his wife did the shooting, since he would have done the deed himself, and more effectively. This episode resolves the tension between Miss Kelly and Mrs. Nordley, ends the relationship between Mrs. Nordley and Marswell, and finally ends the estrangement of Mrs. Nordley from her husband. Also, this dramatic scene clears the air without ever allowing the cuckolded husband, Donald Nordley, to know what was really going on.

The next day, the party breaks camp, leaving Marswell behind to try to capture some young gorillas to pay for the safari. Marswell is able to bring himself to make a proposal of marriage to Miss Kelly but she now rebuffs him. As the canoes are pulling away down the river, she watches him standing on the bank. Suddenly, she jumps into the water and makes her way back to him. The two embrace and the movie ends.

The entire movie turns on this love quadrangle—Kelly-Marswell-Mrs. Nordley-Mr. Nordley—and the contrapostion of the obviousness of the developing affair between Mrs. Nordley and Marswell, and the innocence of Mr. Nordley (even to the point of defending Marswell when another member of Marswell's party tries to inform him).

Production notes

Grace Kelly was not the first choice for the role of Linda Nordley. Gene Tierney dropped out due to her emotional problems. The movie was filmed on location in Okalataka, French Congo; Mount Kenya, Thika, Kenya - you can see Mt Longonot and Lake Naivasha, both in the Kenyan Rift Valley, and Fourteen Falls near Thika as backdrops - Kagera River, Tanganyika; Isoila, Uganda; and at the MGM British Studios, Borehamwood, Hertfordshire, England, UK. The film offers some of the best wildlife shots taken of the African continent, at the time. However there were never gorillas in Kenya so the locations are an odd mix from a naturalist perspective. The music is all performed by local native tribes (except for Gardner accompanied by player piano), unusually for Hollywood, and the film records a traditional Africa that has long since passed.

Subsequently, the Francoist Spanish censors wanted to hide the issue of adultery, and changed the dubbing to make the Nordleys brother and sister. As a result, it appeared to be an even more scandalous case of incest.

Cast

- Clark Gable ... Victor Marswell
- Ava Gardner ... Honey Bear Kelly
- Grace Kelly ... Linda Nordley
- Donald Sinden ... Donald Nordley
- Philip Stainton ... John Brown-Pryce
- Eric Pohlmann ... Leon Boltchak
- Laurence Naismith ... Skipper
- Denis O'Dea ... Father Josef

In popular culture

The theme for *Mogambo* was loosely adapted by Mark Barber for the Auckland University Tramping Club Revue in 1954. A party travelling down the Anawhata on the first Saturday of the May vacation discovered that the cry 'Mogambo' could be produced with great volume and had very satisfactory resonant qualities. It became a club call, of greeting or when making contact on a tramp, for many years.

Murray "Murray the K" Kauffman, popular 1950s and 1960s New York City DJ, used the chant "Ah, Bey, ah bey, koowi zowa zowa" lifted from *Mogambo* as one of his trademark on-air phrases.

Source (edited): "http://en.wikipedia.org/wiki/Mogambo"

Mother Machree

Mother Machree is a 1928 silent film, directed by John Ford, based on a novel by Rida Johnson Young about a poor Irish immigrant in America. John Wayne had a minor role in the film.

Cast

- Belle Bennett as Mother Machree (Ellen McHugh)
- Neil Hamilton as Brian McHugh, aka Brian van Studdiford
- Victor McLaglen as The Giant of Kilkenny (Terence O'Dowd)
- Constance Howard as Edith Cutting
- Philippe De Lacy as Brian McHugh (as a child)
- Ted McNamara as The Harper of Wexford
- Billy Platt as The Dwarf of Munster (Pips) (billed as William Platt)
- Eulalie Jensen as Rachel van Studdiford
- Pat Somerset as Bobby de Puyster
- John Wayne

Preservation

Only 3 reels out 7 of this movie survive, the other 4 are lost.

Source (edited): "http://en.wikipedia.org/wiki/Mother_Machree"

My Darling Clementine

This article is about the John Ford Western. For the song see Oh My Darling, Clementine.

My Darling Clementine

My Darling Clementine is a 1946 western movie. It was directed by John Ford, and based on the story of the Gunfight at the O.K. Corral between the Earp brothers and the Clanton gang. It features an ensemble cast including Henry Fonda, Victor Mature, Ward Bond, Walter Brennan, and others.

The movie was adapted by Samuel G. Engel, Sam Hellman, and Winston Miller from the book *Wyatt Earp: Frontier Marshal* by Stuart N. Lake. The title derives from the folk song "Oh My Darling, Clementine", which is the theme song of the movie (sung in parts over the opening and closing credits). Whole scenes from an earlier version, 1939's *Frontier Marshal*, directed by Alan Dwan, produced by Sol M. Wurtzel, were reshot by Ford for this remake.

In 1991, this film was deemed "culturally, historically, or aesthetically significant" by the Library of Congress and selected for preservation in the United States National Film Registry.

Plot

In 1882 (the wrong year is marked on the tombstone of James, since Oct 26th, 1881 was the date of the Gunfight at the O.K. Corral), the Earp brothers (Wyatt, Morgan, Virgil and James) are driving cattle to California when they cross the Clanton family led by the "Old Man". Told of a nearby town, Tombstone, the older brothers ride in, leaving the youngest brother James to watch over the cattle. The Earps quickly find Tombstone a lawless town. When they return to their camp, they find the cattle rustled and James dead.

Seeking vengeance, Wyatt returns to Tombstone and takes the open job of town marshall, meeting with the local powers, Doc Holliday and the Clantons, again and again in order to find out who was responsible. In the meantime, a young woman from Boston named Clementine Carter arrives in town...

Plot devices

Although the characters and setting of the Gunfight at the O.K. Corral are presented, a great deal of the plot of the film significantly deviates from the actual history. Important plot devices in the film, such as the death of James Earp (who actually died in 1926), the death of Old Man Clanton (who actually died two months *before* the O.K. Corral confrontation), and personal details about Doc Holliday (who was a dentist, not a surgeon, and actually died 6 years later of tuberculosis in Glenwood Springs, Colorado), are inaccurately portrayed.

Production notes

Much of the film was shot in Monument Valley, a scenic desert region straddling the Arizona-Utah border used in other John Ford movies. After holding a preview screening of the film, 20th Century Fox studio boss Darryl F. Zanuck felt Ford's original cut was too long and had some weak spots, so he had Lloyd Bacon shoot new footage and then heavily edited the film. While Ford's original cut of the film has not survived, a "pre-release" cut - dating from a few months after the preview screening - survives with some of Ford's additional footage and alternative score intact.

Cast

- Henry Fonda as Wyatt Earp
- Victor Mature as Dr. John Henry "Doc" Holliday
- Cathy Downs as Clementine Carter, Doc's ex-lover
- Linda Darnell as Chihuahua
- Walter Brennan as Newman Haynes Clanton, cattleman
- Tim Holt as Virgil Earp
- Ward Bond as Morgan Earp
- Don Garner as James Earp
- Grant Withers as Ike Clanton
- John Ireland as Billy Clanton
- Alan Mowbray as Granville Thorndyke, stage actor
- Roy Roberts as Mayor
- Jane Darwell as Kate Nelson
- J. Farrell MacDonald as Mac the barman

Critical reception

Film critic Bosley Crowther lauded the film and wrote, "The eminent director, John Ford, is a man who has a way with a Western like nobody in the picture trade. Seven years ago his classic *Stagecoach* snuggled very close to fine art in this genre. And now, by George, he's almost matched it with *My Darling Clementine*...But even with standard Western fiction—and that's what the script has enjoined—Mr. Ford can evoke fine sensations and curiously-captivating moods. From the moment that Wyatt and his brothers are discovered on the wide and dusty range, trailing a herd of cattle to a far-off promised land, a tone of pictorial authority is struck—and it is held. Every scene, every shot is the product of a keen and sensitive eye—an eye which has deep comprehension of the beauty of rugged people and a rugged world".

The staff at *Variety* magazine wrote of the film, "Trademark of John Ford's direction is clearly stamped on the film with its shadowy lights, softly contrasted moods and measured pace, but a tendency is discernible towards stylization for stylization's sake. At several points, the pic comes to a dead stop to let Ford go gunning for some arty effect".

Director Sam Peckinpah considered *My Darling Clementine* his favorite Western, and paid homage to it in several of his Westerns, including *Major Dundee* (1965) and *The Wild Bunch* (1969).

In the popular TV series, *M*A*S*H*, Colonel Potter's favourite film is *My Darling Clementine*. Clips from the film are shown in the season 5 episode, "Movie Tonight".

The film currently holds a 100% fresh rating on Rotten Tomatoes.

Source (edited): "http://en.wikipedia.org/wiki/My_Darling_Clementine"

Napoleon's Barber

Napoleon's Barber is a 1928 short drama film directed by John Ford. The film is considered to be lost.

Cast

- Otto Matieson - Napoleon
- Natalie Golitzen - Empress Josephine
- Frank Reicher - Napoleon's Barber
- Helen Ware - The Barber's Wife
- Philippe De Lacy - The Barber's Son
- D'Arcy Corrigan - Tailor
- Russ Powell - Blacksmith
- Michael Mark - Peasant
- Buddy Roosevelt - French Officer
- Ervin Renard - French Officer
- Youcca Troubetzkoy - French Officer
- Joseph Waddell - French Officer
- Henry Hebert - Soldier

Source (edited): "http://en.wikipedia.org/wiki/Napoleon%27s_Barber"

North of Hudson Bay

North of Hudson Bay is a 1923 action film directed by John Ford. Approximately 40 minutes of footage still exist.

Cast

- Tom Mix - Michael Dane
- Kathleen Key - Estelle McDonald
- Jennie Lee - Dane's mother
- Frank Campeau - Cameron McDonald
- Eugene Pallette - Peter Dane
- Will Walling - Angus McKenzie
- Frank Leigh - Jeffrey Clough
- Fred Kohler - Armand LeMoir

Source (edited): "http://en.wikipedia.org/wiki/North_of_Hudson_Bay"

Pilgrimage (1933 film)

Pilgrimage is a 1933 drama film directed by John Ford.

Cast

- Henrietta Crosman - Mrs. Hannah Jessop
- Heather Angel - Suzanne
- Norman Foster - Jim 'Jimmy' Jessop (Hannah's son)
- Lucille La Verne - Mrs. Kelly Hatfield
- Maurice Murphy - Gary Worth
- Marian Nixon - Mary Saunders
- Jay Ward - Jimmy Saunders (Mary and Jimmy Hessop's son)
- Robert Warwick - Major Albertson
- Louise Carter - Mrs. Rogers
- Betty Blythe - Janet Prescot
- Francis Ford - Mayor Elmer Briggs
- Charley Grapewin - Dad Saunders
- Hedda Hopper - Mrs. Worth (Gary Worth's mother)
- Frances Rich - The Nurse

Source (edited): "http://en.wikipedia.org/wiki/Pilgrimage_(1933_film)"

Rider of the Law

Rider of the Law is a 1919 Western film directed by John Ford and featuring Harry Carey. The film is considered to be lost.

Cast

- Harry Carey - Jim Kyneton
- Vester Pegg - Nick Kyneton (as Vesta Pegg)
- Ted Brooks - The Kid
- Joe Harris - Buck Soutar
- Jack Woods - Jack West
- Duke R. Lee - Captain Saltire (as Duke Lee)
- Gloria Hope - Betty
- Claire Anderson -Roseen
- Jennie Lee - Jim's Mother

Source (edited): "http://en.wikipedia.org/wiki/Rider_of_the_Law"

Riders of Vengeance

Riders of Vengeance is a 1919 Western film directed by John Ford and featuring Harry Carey. The film is considered to be lost.

Production

Riders of Vengeance was released as a Universal Special feature in June 1919, a 60-minute silent film on six reels. It was part of the long-running "Cheyenne Harry" series of film featurettes. The story was an uncommon collaboration between the star Harry Carey and the director John Ford (with help from scenarist Eugene Lewis). Though it has an unusually high level of violence ("lots of killings", as *Moving Picture World* noted), critical reviews of the time lavishly praised both the story and film.

Plot

Harry's bride is murdered at their wedding, and the good-hearted outlaw turns grimly malevolent. One by one he stalks his wife's killers, dispatching them all until he finally sets his sights, mistakenly, on Sheriff Gale Thurman. The lawman bests Harry and keeps him hiding outside town in the wilderness. Straying into the same wilderness, the Sheriff's girlfriend is first overtaken by highwaymen, then rescued by Harry, only to be taken captive by Harry when he realizes who she is. At first threatening to harm the girl, Harry slowly falls in love with her, all while hostile Apaches attempt to kill them both. By the time the Sheriff tracks them down, a full-scale assault is under way, and the two men join forces. Harry realizes the Sheriff's innocence, but it is too late: the lawman is dead from his battle wounds, but he has saved his girlfriend - and Harry.

Cast

- Harry Carey - Cheyenne Harry
- Seena Owen - The Girl
- Joe Harris - Gale Thurman (as Joseph Harris)
- J. Farrell MacDonald - Buell
- Alfred Allen - Harry's Father
- Jennie Lee - Harry's Mother
- Clita Gale - Virginia
- Vester Pegg
- Betty Schade
- Millard K. Wilson - (as M.K. Wilson)

Source (edited): "http://en.wikipedia.org/wiki/Riders_of_Vengeance"

Riley the Cop

Riley the Cop is a 1928 comedy film directed by John Ford. It was a silent film with a synchronized music track.

Cast

- J. Farrell MacDonald - James 'Aloysius' Riley (as Farrell Macdonald)
- Nancy Drexel - Mary Coronelli
- David Rollins - David 'Davy' Collins
- Louise Fazenda - Lena Krausmeyer
- Billy Bevan - Paris Cabman (uncredited)
- Mildred Boyd - Caroline (uncredited)
- Mike Donlin - Crook (uncredited)
- Otto Fries - Munich Cabman (uncredited)
- Dell Henderson - Judge Coronelli (uncredited)
- Isabelle Keith - French Woman on Pier (uncredited)
- Robert Parrish - Boy (uncredited)
- Russ Powell - Mr. Kuchendorf (uncredited)
- Harry Schultz - Hans 'Eitel' Krausmeyer (uncredited)
- Ferdinand Schumann-Heink - Julius Kuchendorf (uncredited)
- Rolfe Sedan - French Restaurant Patron (uncredited)
- Harry Semels - French Policeman (uncredited)
- Tom Wilson - Sergeant (uncredited)

Source (edited): "http://en.wikipedia.org/wiki/Riley_the_Cop"

Rio Grande (film)

Rio Grande is a 1950 western film. It is the third installment of John Ford's "cavalry trilogy," following two RKO Pictures releases: *Fort Apache* (1948) and *She Wore a Yellow Ribbon* (1949).

John Wayne stars in all three films, as Captain Kirby Yorke in *Fort Apache*, then as Captain of Cavalry Nathan Cutting Brittles in *She Wore a Yellow Ribbon*, and finally as a promoted Lieutenant Colonel Kirby Yorke in *Rio Grande* (scripts and production billing spell the York/Yorke character's last name differently in *Fort Apache* and *Rio Grande*).

The film is based on a short story "Mission With No Record" by James Warner Bellah, that appeared in *The Saturday Evening Post* on September 27, 1947, and the screenplay was written by James Kevin McGuinness.

Production

Ford wanted to make *The Quiet Man* first, but Republic Pictures studio president Herbert Yates, insisted that Ford make *Rio Grande* first, using the same combination of Wayne and Maureen O'Hara; Yates did not feel that the script of *The Quiet Man* was very good, and wanted *Rio Grande* to be released first to pay for *The Quiet Man*. To Yates's surprise *The Quiet Man,* on its eventual release in 1952, would become Republic's number one film in terms of box office receipts.

Maureen O'Hara starred with John Wayne in 5 movies: *Rio Grande* (1950), *The Quiet Man* (1952), *The Wings of Eagles* (1957), *McLintock!* (1963) and *Big Jake* (1971). The first three were directed by John Ford.

This was the film debut of Patrick Wayne.

The film was shot in Monument Valley, and other locations in southeastern Utah around the town of Moab and along the Colorado River.

Plot

In *Rio Grande*, Lt. Col. Kirby Yorke is posted on the Texas frontier to defend settlers against depredations of marauding Apaches. Col. Yorke is under considerable stress between the Apaches using Mexico as a sanctuary from pursuit and by a serious shortage of troops of his command.

Tension is added when Yorke's son (whom he hasn't seen in fifteen years), Trooper Jeff Yorke (Claude Jarman Jr.), is one of 18 recruits sent to the regiment. He has flunked out of West Point and immediately enlisted as a private in the Army. Not wanting to give any impression that he is showing favoritism towards his son, Col. Yorke ends up being harsher dealing with Jeff than the others. By his willingness to undergo any test and trial, Jeff is befriended by a pair of older recruits, Travis Tyree (Ben Johnson) (who is on the run from the law) and "Sandy" Boone (Harry Carey,

Jr.), who take him under their wings.

With the arrival of Yorke's estranged wife, Kathleen (Maureen O'Hara), who has come to take the under-age Yorke home with her, further tension is added. During the war, Yorke had been forced by circumstances to burn Bridesdale, his wife's plantation home in the Shenandoah valley. Sgt. Quincannon (Victor McLaglen), who put the torch to Bridesdale, is still with Yorke and provides a constant reminder to Kathleen of the episode. In a showdown with his mother, Jeff refuses her attempt by reminding her that not only the commander's signature is required to discharge him, but his own as well, and he chooses to stay in the Army. The tension brought about in the struggle over their son's future (and possibly the attentions shown to her by Yorke's junior officers) rekindles the romance the couple once felt for each other.

Yorke is visited by his former Civil War commander, Philip Sheridan (J. Carrol Naish), now commanding general of his department. Sheridan has decided to order Yorke to cross the Rio Grande into Mexico in pursuit of the Apaches, an action with serious political implications since it violates the sovereignty of another nation.

If Yorke fails in his mission to destroy the Apache threat he faces the threat of court-martial. Sheridan, in a quiet act of acknowledgment of what he is asking Yorke to risk, promises that the members of the court will be men "who rode down the Shenandoah" with them during the Civil War. Yorke accepts the mission. Now Col. Yorke must fight to save, and put back together, his family and his honor.

Yorke leads his men toward Mexico, only to learn that a wagonload of children from his fort, who were being taken to Ft. Bliss for safety, has been captured by the Apaches. After permitting a small detachment of troopers—including Yorke's son, Jeff—to scout out the Mexican village where the Indians have taken the children, Yorke leads his cavalry in a full-scale attack, rescuing all of the children unharmed but being wounded himself. He is taken back to the fort by his victorious troops, where Kathleen meets him and holds his hand as he is carried (on a travois into the post as the movie closes.

Basis

Some aspects of the story, notably the regiment's crossing into Mexico, and undertaking a campaign there, loosely resemble the expedition conducted by the 4th Cavalry Regiment (United States) under Colonel Ranald S. Mackenzie in 1873.

Music

The film contains folk songs led by the Sons of the Pioneers, one of which is Ken Curtis (Ford's son-in-law and best known for his role as Festus Haggen on *Gunsmoke*).

Source (edited): "http://en.wikipedia.org/wiki/Rio_Grande_(film)"

Roped

Roped is a 1919 Western film directed by John Ford and featuring Harry Carey. The film is considered to be lost.

Cast

- Harry Carey - Cheyenne Harry
- Neva Gerber - Aileen
- Mollie McConnell - Mrs. Judson-Brown (as Molly McConnell)
- Arthur Shirley - Ferdie Van Duzen
- J. Farrell MacDonald - Butler

Source (edited): "http://en.wikipedia.org/wiki/Roped"

Rustlers (film)

Rustlers is a 1919 short Western film directed by John Ford.

Cast

- Pete Morrison
- Helen Gibson
- Hoot Gibson
- Jack Woods

Source (edited): "http://en.wikipedia.org/wiki/Rustlers_(film)"

Salute (film)

Salute is a 1929 motion picture directed by John Ford, starring George O'Brien, Helen Chandler, William Janney, Stepin Fetchit (Lincoln Perry), and Frank Albertson about the football rivalry of the Army–Navy Game, and of two brothers, played by O'Brien and Janney, one of West Point, the other of Annapolis. John Wayne had an uncredited role in the film, as one of three midshipmen who perform a mild hazing. The film was partly filmed on location at Annapolis Naval Academy. The comic relief character played by Fetchit was common for the era, but is extremely racist and degrading by today's standards.

Cast

- George O'Brien as Cadet John Randall
- Helen Chandler as Nancy Wayne
- William Janney as Midshipman Paul Randall
- Stepin Fetchit as Smoke Screen
- Frank Albertson as Brian Midshipman Albert Edward Price

Seas Beneath

Seas Beneath is a 1931 action film directed by John Ford.

Cast
- George O'Brien - Cmdr. Robert 'Bob' Kingsley
- Marion Lessing - Anna Marie Von Steuben
- Mona Maris - Fraulein Lolita
- Walter C. Kelly - Chief Mike 'Guns' Costello
- Warren Hymer - 'Lug' Kaufman
- Steve Pendleton - Ens. Richard 'Dick' Cabot (as Gaylord Pendleton)
- Walter McGrail - Chief Joe Cobb
- Larry Kent - Lt. 'Mac' McGregor
- Henry Victor - Baron Ernst von Steuben (U-boat commander)
- John Loder - Franz Shiller

Source (edited): "http://en.wikipedia.org/wiki/Seas_Beneath"

Sergeant Rutledge

Sergeant Rutledge is a 1960 Western and military courtroom drama starring Woody Strode and Jeffrey Hunter. It was directed by John Ford and shot on location in Monument Valley, Utah.

The film starred Strode as a black first sergeant in the United States Cavalry accused of the rape and murder of a white girl at a U.S. Army fort in the late 1880s.

Plot

The film revolves around the court-martial of 1st Sgt. Braxton Rutledge (Strode), a "Buffalo Soldier" of the 9th U.S. Cavalry. His defense is handled by Lt. Tom Cantrell (Hunter), Rutledge's troop officer. The story is told through a series of flashbacks, expanding the testimony of witnesses as they describe the events following the murder of Rutledge's Commanding Officer, Major Dabney, and the rape and murder of Dabney's daughter, for which Rutledge is the accused.

Circumstantial evidence suggests that the first sergeant raped and murdered the girl and then killed his commanding officer. Worse still, Rutledge deserts after the killings. Ultimately, he is tracked down arrested by Lt. Cantrell. At one point, Rutledge escapes from captivity during an Indian raid, but later, he voluntarily returns to warn his fellow cavalrymen that they are about to face an ambush, thus saving the troop. He then is then brought back in to face the charges and the prejudices of an all-white military court.

Eventually he is found not guilty of the rape and murder of the girl when a local white man breaks down under questioning to admit that he raped the girl.

Cast
- Jeffrey Hunter as 1st Lt. Tom Cantrell, 9th Cavalry (counsel for the defense)
- Constance Towers as Mary Beecher
- Billie Burke as Mrs. Cordelia Fosgate
- Woody Strode as First Sergeant Braxton Rutledge, 9th Cavalry
- Juano Hernández as Sgt. Matthew Luke Skidmore, 9th Cavalry
- Willis Bouchey as Lt. Col. Otis Fosgate, 9th Cavalry (president of the court-martial)
- Carleton Young as Capt. Shattuck, 14th Infantry (prosecutor)
- Judson Pratt as 2nd Lt. Mulqueen, 9th Cavalry (court-martial board member)

Source (edited): "http://en.wikipedia.org/wiki/Sergeant_Rutledge"

Sex Hygiene

Sex Hygiene is a 1942 documentary film directed by John Ford and Otto Brower. It belonged to the instructional social guidance film genre, which offered adolescent and adult behavioural advice, medical information and moral exhortations.

Plot

Several servicemen relax through playing pool at their base. One later visits a sex worker and contracts syphilis. As a result of his unfortunate experience, there is an opportunity for sexual health information about syphilis, how it is spread and how its spread can be prevented.

Cast
- Kenneth Alexander - Soldier
- Robert Conway - Soldier
- Robert Cornell - Soldier
- Richard Derr - Soldier
- Herbert Gunn - Soldier
- Robert Lowery - Pool player #2
- George Reeves - Pool player #1
- Robert Shaw - Pool player
- Charles Tannen - Soldier
- Charles Trowbridge - Medical officer
- Basil Walker - Soldier
- Robert Weldon - Soldier

Source (edited): "http://en.wikipedia.org/wiki/Sex_Hygiene"

She Wore a Yellow Ribbon

She Wore a Yellow Ribbon is a 1949 western film directed by John Ford and starring John Wayne. The film was the second of Ford's trilogy of films focusing on the US Cavalry (and the only one in color); the other two films were *Fort Apache* (1948) and *Rio Grande* (1950). With a budget of $1.6 million, the film was one of the most expensive westerns of the time, but became a major hit for RKO and remains a popular classic today.

Known for its breathtaking views of Monument Valley located in the Navajo reservation, at the northern edge of Arizona; the cinematographer, Winton Hoch, won the 1950 Academy Award for Best Color Cinematography. Ford and Hoch based much of the film's imagery on the paintings and sculptures of Frederic Remington.

The film is named after a song common in the U.S. military, "She Wore a Yellow Ribbon", which is still used today to keep marching cadence. It is a variant of the song "All Around My Hat".

Plot

On the verge of his retirement at Fort Starke, a one-troop cavalry post, the aging US Cavalry Capt. Nathan Cutting Brittles (John Wayne) is given one last patrol, to take his troop and deal with a breakout from the reservation by the Cheyenne and Arapaho following the defeat of George Armstrong Custer. His task is complicated by being forced at the same time to deliver his commanding officer's wife and niece, Abby Allshard (Mildred Natwick) and Olivia Dandridge (Joanne Dru), to an eastbound stage, and by the need to avoid a new Indian war. His troop officers, 1st Lt. Flint Cohill (John Agar) and 2nd Lt. Ross Pennell (Harry Carey, Jr.) meanwhile vie for the affections of Miss Dandridge while uneasily anticipating the retirement of their captain and mentor. Rounding out the cast are Capt. Brittles' chief scout, Sgt. Tyree (Ben Johnson), a one-time Confederate cavalry officer; his First Sergeant, Quincannon (Victor McLaglen); and Major Allshard (George O'Brien), long-time friend and commanding officer.

After apparently failing in both missions, Capt. Brittles returns with the troop to Fort Starke to retire. His lieutenants continue the mission in the field, joined by Capt. Brittles after "quitting the post and the Army". Unwilling to see more lives needlessly taken, Capt. Brittles takes it upon himself to try to make peace with Chief Pony That Walks (Chief John Big Tree). When that too fails, he devises a risky stratagem to avoid a bloody war by stampeding the Indians' horses out of the camp and back to the reservation.

The movie ends with Brittles being recalled to duty as chief of scouts with the rank of lieutenant-colonel and miss Dandridge and lieutenant Cohill becoming engaged.

Errors

The film's narrator references Pony Express rider's concerns over George Custer's defeat at the Battle of the Little Bighorn. Custer was killed in 1876, whereas the Pony Express made its last ride fifteen years earlier in 1861 after only a year of service.

Cast

Nathan Brittles house in the movie

Other Cast

- Rudy Bowman as Trooper John Smith aka Brig. Gen. Rome Clay, CSA (uncredited)
- Lee Bradley as Interpreter (uncredited)
- Paul Fix as Gun-runner (uncredited)
- Francis Ford as Connelly, Fort Stark Suttlers Barman (uncredited)
- Ray Hyke as Trooper McCarthy (uncredited)
- Billy Jones as Courier (uncredited)
- Fred Kennedy as Badger (uncredited)
- Fred Libby as Cpl. Krumrein (uncredited)
- Cliff Lyons as Trooper Cliff (uncredited)
- Frank McGrath as Bugler / Indian (uncredited)
- Peter Ortiz as Gun-runner (uncredited)
- Post Park as Officer (uncredited)
- Jack Pennick as Sergeant Major (uncredited)
- Mickey Simpson as Cpl. Wagner (blacksmith) (uncredited)
- William Steele as Officer (uncredited)
- Don Summers as Jenkins (uncredited)
- Dan White as Trooper (uncredited)
- Harry Woods as Licensed Suttler Karl Rynders (uncredited)

Source (edited): "http://en.wikipedia.org/wiki/She_Wore_a_Yellow_Ribbon"

Silver Wings (film)

Silver Wings is a 1922 drama film directed by Edwin Carewe and John Ford. The film is considered to be lost.

Cast

- Mary Carr - Anna Webb (prologue / play)
- Lynn Hammond - John Webb (prologue)
- Knox Kincaid - John (prologue)
- Joseph Monahan - Harry (prologue)
- Maybeth Carr - Ruth (prologue)
- Claude Brooke - Uncle Andrews (prologue / play)
- Robert Hazelton - The Minister (prologue)
- Florence Short - Widow Martin (prologue)
- May Kaiser - Her Child
- Percy Helton - John (play)
- Joseph Striker - Harry (play)
- Jane Thomas - Ruth (play)
- Roy Gordon - George Mills (play)
- Florence Haas - Little Anna (play)
- L. Rogers Lytton - Bank President (play) (as Roger Lytton)
- Ernest Hilliard - Jerry Gibbs (play)

Source (edited): "http://en.wikipedia.org/wiki/Silver_Wings_(film)"

Stagecoach (1939 film)

Stagecoach is a 1939 American Western film directed by John Ford, starring Claire Trevor and John Wayne in his breakthrough role. The screenplay, written by Dudley Nichols and Ben Hecht, is an adaptation of "The Stage to Lordsburg", a 1937 short story by Ernest Haycox. The film follows a group of strangers riding on a stagecoach through dangerous Apache territory.

Although Ford had made many westerns in the silent film era, he had never directed a sound western. Between 1929–1939, he directed films of almost every other genre, including *Wee Willie Winkie* (1937) starring Shirley Temple. *Stagecoach* was to be his first sound western and the first of many that Ford made on location in Monument Valley, in the American southwest on the Arizona-Utah border, many of which also starred John Wayne.

Plot

In 1880, a motley group of strangers boards the east-bound stagecoach from Tonto, Arizona Territory to Lordsburg, New Mexico Territory. Among them are Dallas (Claire Trevor), a prostitute who is being driven out of town by the members of the "Law and Order League"; an alcoholic doctor, Doc Boone (Thomas Mitchell); Lucy Mallory (Louise Platt), who is traveling to see her cavalry officer husband; and whiskey salesman Samuel Peacock (Donald Meek).

When the stage driver, Buck (Andy Devine), looks for his normal shotgun guard, he is told by Marshal Curly Wilcox (George Bancroft) that he has gone out to look for a fugitive, the Ringo Kid (John Wayne). Buck tells Marshal Wilcox that Luke Plummer (Tom Tyler) is in Lordsburg. Knowing that the Kid has vowed to avenge the deaths of his father and brother at Plummer's hands, the marshal decides to ride along.

As they start to pull out, U.S. cavalry Lieutenant Blanchard (Tim Holt) informs them that Geronimo and his Apaches are on the warpath. His small troop will provide an escort until they get to Dry Fork. Gambler and Southern gentleman Hatfield (John Carradine) joins them to provide protection for Mrs. Mallory. At the edge of town, the stage is flagged down by pompous banker Henry Gatewood, (Berton Churchill), who is sneaking away with $50,000 embezzled from his bank.

Along the way, they come across Henry "The Ringo Kid" (John Wayne), whose horse had become lame and left him afoot. Even though they are friends, Curly has no choice but to take Ringo into custody. As the trip progresses, Ringo takes a strong liking to Dallas.

When they reach Dry Fork, they are informed that the expected cavalry detachment has moved on to Apache Wells. The passengers vote on whether to press on or turn back. With only Peacock objecting, they go on and reach Apache Wells. There, Mrs. Mallory faints when she hears that her husband had been wounded in battle. She begins to go into labor. Doc Boone is called upon to help her through her childbirth. Eventually, Dallas emerges with a healthy baby. Later that night, Ringo asks Dallas to marry him. She does not give him an immediate answer, afraid to reveal her checkered past, but the next morning, she agrees to marry him if he promises to give up his plan to take on the Plummers. Encouraged by Dallas, Ringo makes a break for it, but turns back when he sees signs of Indians.

When they reach Lee's Ferry, they find the station and the ferry burned down and the people either dead or having fled. They tie large logs to each side of the stagecoach and float it across the river. Just when they think that they are in the clear, the stagecoach is chased by the Apaches. Curly releases the Kid from his handcuffs to help fight them off. During a long chase, when things look bleak, Hatfield is about to kill Mrs. Mallory with his last bullet to save her from being taken alive when he is fatally wounded. Just then, the 6th U.S. cavalry charges to the rescue.

When the passengers finally arrive in Lordsburg, Gatewood is arrested by the local sheriff, and Lucy is told that her husband's wound is not serious. Dallas begs Ringo not to go up against the Plummers, but he is determined to settle matters and Curly grants him leave and his gun to go looking for them. In the ensuing shootout, the Kid dispatches Luke and his two brothers. He returns to Wilcox, expecting to go back to jail. He asks the lawman to take Dallas to his ranch. However, when Ringo gets on a wagon to say goodbye to her, Curly invites her aboard to ride a ways out of town with Ringo. She climbs up with Ringo, and Curly and Doc laugh and start the horses moving, letting him "escape" with Dallas.

Cast

- Claire Trevor as Dallas
- John Wayne as The Ringo Kid

- Andy Devine as Buck
- John Carradine as Hatfield
- Thomas Mitchell as Doc Boone
- Louise Platt as Lucy Mallory
- George Bancroft as Marshal Curly Wilcox
- Donald Meek as Samuel Peacock
- Berton Churchill as Henry Gatewood
- Tim Holt as Lieutenant Blanchard
- Tom Tyler as Luke Plummer
- Yakima Canutt as Cavalry scout, uncredited stunt coordinator and second unit director
- Chris-Pin Martin as Chris
- Chief White Horse as Geronimo

Origins

The screenplay is an adaptation by Dudley Nichols of "The Stage to Lordsburg," a short story by Ernest Haycox. The rights to "Lordsburg" were bought by John Ford soon after it was published in *Collier's* magazine on 10 April 1937. According to Thomas Schatz, Ford claimed that his inspiration in expanding *Stagecoach* beyond the barebones plot given in "The Stage to Lordsburg" was his familiarity with another short story, "Boule de Suif" by Guy de Maupassant. Schatz believes "this scarcely holds up to scrutiny" and argues that a more likely inspiration was Bret Harte's 1892 short story "*The Outcasts of Poker Flat*."

Ford's statement also seems to be the basis for the claim that Haycox himself relied upon Guy de Maupassant's story. However, there appears to be no concrete evidence for Haycox actually being familiar with the earlier story, especially as he was documented as going out of his way to avoid reading the work of others that might unconsciously influence his writing, and he focused his personal reading in the area of history.

Pre-production

Although they were close friends, Ford had declined to use Wayne in any of his projects during the 1930s, telling him to wait until he was "ready" as an actor. In 1938 he gave Wayne a copy of the film's script by Nichols, asking him to recommend an actor to play the Ringo Kid. After having read it, Wayne suggested Lloyd Nolan for the part, but Ford was non-committal to the idea. The next day however, Ford announced to Wayne that he wanted *him* to play the role. The offer left Wayne feeling as if he had been "hit in the belly with a baseball bat"...and fearing that Ford would change his mind and hire Nolan instead.

Before production, John Ford shopped the project around to several Hollywood studios, all of which turned him down because big budget Westerns were out of vogue, and because Ford insisted on using John Wayne in a key role in the film. Wayne had appeared in only one big-budget western, *The Big Trail* (1930, directed by Raoul Walsh), which was a huge box office flop. Between 1930–1939, by Wayne's own estimate, he appeared in about eighty "Poverty Row" westerns. Independent producer David O. Selznick finally agreed to produce the film, but frustrated Ford with his indecisiveness over when shooting should begin, as well as Selznick's doubts over the casting. Ford withdrew the film from Selznick's company, then approached independent producer Walter Wanger about the project. Wanger had the same reservations about producing an "A" western and even more about one starring John Wayne. Ford had not directed a western since the silent days, the most notable of which had been *The Iron Horse* (1924). Wanger said he would not risk his money unless Ford replaced John Wayne with Gary Cooper and brought in Marlene Dietrich to play Dallas.

Ford refused to budge; it would be Wayne or no one. Eventually they compromised, with Wanger putting up $250,000, a little more than half of what Ford had been asking for, and Ford would give top billing to Claire Trevor, a far better-known name than John Wayne in 1939.

Reception

Stagecoach has been lauded as one of the most influential films ever made. Orson Welles argued that it was a perfect textbook of film making and claimed to have watched it more than 40 times during the making of *Citizen Kane*.

Awards and honors

Wins

- Academy Award for Best Supporting Actor - Thomas Mitchell
- Academy Award for Best Music, Scoring - Richard Hageman, W. Franke Harling, John Leipold, Leo Shuken
- New York Film Critics Circle Awards for Best Director - John Ford

Nominations

- Academy Award for Best Picture
- Academy Award for Directing - John Ford
- Academy Award for Best Art Direction - Alexander Toluboff
- Academy Award for Best Cinematography-Black-and-White - Bert Glennon
- Academy Award for Film Editing - Otho Lovering, Dorothy Spencer

Others

- John Ford won the 1939 New York Film Critics Award as Best Director. Other critics gave the film uniformly glowing reviews.
- In 1995, this film was deemed "culturally, historically, or aesthetically significant" by the United States Library of Congress and selected for preservation in their National Film Registry.
- In June 2008, the American Film Institute revealed its "Ten Top Ten"—the best ten films in ten "classic" American film genres—after polling over 1,500 people from the creative community. *Stagecoach* was acknowledged as the ninth best film in the western genre.

Re-releases and restoration

The film was originally released through United Artists, but under their old seven-year-rights rule, surrendered its distribution rights to producer Walter Wanger in 1946. Many independent companies were responsible for this film in the years since. The film's copyright (originally by Walter Wanger Productions) was renewed by 20th Century Fox, who produced a later 1966 remake of *Stagecoach*. The copyright has since been reassigned to Wanger Productions through his family under the Caidin Trust/Caidin Film Company, the ancillary rights holder. However, distribution rights are now held by the UCLA Film and Television Archive on behalf of Caidin, represented by Westchester Films (which had acquired the Caidin Film holdings after the folding of former distributor Castle Hill Productions). Warner Bros. Pictures handles sales and additional distribution.

The original negatives of *Stagecoach* were either lost or destroyed. John Wayne had one positive print that had never been through a projector gate. In 1970, he permitted it to be used to produce a new negative, and that is the film seen today at film festivals. UCLA formally restored the film in 1996 from surviving elements and premiered on cable's American Movie Classics network. The previous DVD releases by Warner Home Video did not contain the restored print, but rather a video print held in the Castle Hill/Caidin Trust library. A digitally restored Blu-ray/DVD version was released in May 2010 via The Criterion Collection.

Remakes

- The May 4, 1946 radio episode of Academy Award Theater had Claire Trevor reprise her role alongside Randolph Scott.
- The January 9, 1949 radio episode of Screen Director's Playhouse had John Wayne and Claire Trevor both reprise their parts.
- The 1966 remake of *Stagecoach* starred (in alphabetical order) Ann-Margret, Red Buttons, Mike Connors, Alex Cord, Bing Crosby, Robert Cummings, Van Heflin, Slim Pickens, and Stefanie Powers.
- A 1986 television version featured Willie Nelson, Kris Kristofferson, Johnny Cash, and Waylon Jennings.

Source (edited): "http://en.wikipedia.org/wiki/Stagecoach_(1939_film)"

Steamboat Round the Bend

Steamboat Round the Bend is a 1935 comedy film directed by John Ford.

Plot

A con man enters his steamboat in a winner-take-all race with a rival while attempting to find a witness that will save his nephew, who has been wrongly convicted of murder, from the gallows.

Cast

- Will Rogers - Doctor John Pearly
- Anne Shirley - Fleety Belle
- Irvin S. Cobb - Captain Eli
- Eugene Pallette - Sheriff Rufe Jeffers
- John McGuire - Duke
- Berton Churchill - New Moses
- Francis Ford - Efe
- Roger Imhof - Breck's Pappy
- Raymond Hatton - Matt Abel
- Hobart Bosworth - Chaplain
- Stepin Fetchit - Jonah

Source (edited): "http://en.wikipedia.org/wiki/Steamboat_Round_the_Bend"

Straight Shooting

Straight Shooting is a 1917 Western film directed by John Ford and featuring Harry Carey. Prints of this film survive in the International Museum of Photography and Film at George Eastman House.

Cast

- Harry Carey - Cheyenne Harry
- Duke R. Lee - Thunder Flint (as Duke Lee)
- George Berrell - Sweet Water Sims
- Molly Malone - Joan Sims
- Ted Brooks - Ted Sims
- Hoot Gibson - Danny Morgan (credits)/Sam Turner (titles)
- Milton Brown - Black-Eyed Pete (as Milt Brown)
- Vester Pegg - Placer Fremont

Source (edited): "http://en.wikipedia.org/wiki/Straight_Shooting"

Strong Boy

Strong Boy (1929) is a comedy film directed by John Ford. It was a silent film with a synchronized music track. The film is now considered to be a lost film. A trailer for the film was discovered in the New Zealand Film Archive in 2010.

Cast

- Victor McLaglen - Strong Boy
- Leatrice Joy - Mary McGregor
- J. Farrell MacDonald - Angus McGregor
- Clyde Cook - Pete
- Buddy Roosevelt - Wilbur Watkins (as Kent Sanderson)
- Douglas Scott - Wobby
- Slim Summerville - Slim
- Tom Wilson - Baggage master
- Eulalie Jensen - Queen of Lisonia
- David Torrence - Railroad president
- Dolores Johnson - Prima donna
- Robert Ryan - Baggage man
- Jack Pennick - Baggage man

Source (edited): "http://en.wikipedia.org/wiki/Strong_Boy"

Submarine Patrol

Submarine Patrol is a 1938 film starring Richard Greene and Nancy Kelly. The supporting cast includes Preston Foster and George Bancroft. The movie was partly written by William Faulkner and directed by John Ford.

Cast

Richard Greene ... Perry Townsend III
Nancy Kelly ... Susan Leeds
Preston Foster ... John C. Drake
George Bancroft ... Captain Leeds
Slim Summerville ... Spuds Fickett
J. Farrell MacDonald ... Sails Quincannon
Warren Hymer ... Rocky Haggerty
Douglas Fowley ... Pinky Brett
Dick Hogan ... Johnny Miller
Elisha Cook, Jr. ... Rutherford Davis Pratt ("The Professor")
George E. Stone ... Irving Goldfarb
Jack Pennick ... Guns McPeek
John Carradine ... McAllison
Henry Armetta ... Luigi
Joan Valerie ... Anne

Source (edited): "http://en.wikipedia.org/wiki/Submarine_Patrol"

Sure Fire

Sure Fire is a 1921 Western film directed by John Ford and featuring Hoot Gibson. The film is considered to be lost.

Cast

- Hoot Gibson - Jeff Bransford
- Molly Malone - Marian Hoffman
- B. Reeves Eason Jr. - Sonny (as Breezy Eason Jr.)
- Harry Carter - Rufus Coulter
- Fritzi Brunette - Elinor Parker
- Murdock MacQuarrie - Major Parker
- George Fisher - Burt Rawlings
- Charles Newton - Leo Ballinger
- Jack Woods - Brazos Bart
- Jack Walters - Overland Kid
- Joe Harris - Romero
- Steve Clemente - Gomez (as Steve Clements)
- Mary Philbin

Source (edited): "http://en.wikipedia.org/wiki/Sure_Fire"

Thank You (1925 film)

Thank You is a 1925 comedy film directed by John Ford. The film is considered to be lost.

Cast

- Alec B. Francis - David Lee
- Jacqueline Logan - Diane Lee
- George O'Brien - Kenneth Jamieson
- J. Farrell MacDonald - Andy
- George Fawcett - Cornelius Jamieson
- Cyril Chadwick - Mr. Jones
- Edith Bostwick - Mrs. Jones
- Marion Harlan - Milly Jones
- Vivia Ogden - Miss Blodgett
- James Neill - Doctor Cobb
- Billy Rinaldi - Sweet, Jr.
- Aileen Manning - Hannah
- Maurice Murphy - Willie Jones
- Robert Milasch - Sweet, Sr.
- Ida Moore - Gossiping Woman
- Frankie Bailey - Gossiping Man
- William Courtright (uncredited)
- Richard Cummings (uncredited)
- Tommy Hicks - Fat kid (uncredited)

Source (edited): "http://en.wikipedia.org/wiki/Thank_You_(1925_film)"

The Adventures of Marco Polo

The Adventures of Marco Polo is a 1938 drama-adventure genre film, and one of the most elaborate and costly of Samuel Goldwyn's productions.

Plot

Nicolo Polo shows treasures from China and sends his son Marco Polo (Gary Cooper) there with his assistant (and comic relief) Binguccio (Ernest Truex). They sail from Venice, are shipwrecked, and cross the desert of Persia and the mountains of Tibet to China, to seek out Peking and the palace of China's ruler, Kublai Khan (George Barbier).

The philosopher/fireworks-maker Chen Tsu (H. B. Warner) is the first friend they make in the city, and invites them into his home for a meal of spaghetti. Children explode a firecracker, and Marco thinks it could be a weapon. Meanwhile, at the Palace, Ahmed (Basil Rathbone), the Emperor's adviser, harboring dubious ambitions of his own, convinces Emperor Kublai Khan that his army of a million men can conquer Japan.

Kublai Khan promises Princess Kukachin (Sigrid Gurie) to the King of Persia. Marco, arriving at the palace, sees Kukachin praying for a handsome husband. Marco is granted an audience with the emperor at the same time as a group of ladies-in-waiting arrive; Kublai Khan lets Marco test the maidens to find out which are the most worthy. Marco tests them all with a question ("How many teeth does a snapping turtle have?"), and he sends off the ones who had incorrectly guessed the answer, as well as those who had told him the correct answer (none), retaining those saying they did not know. His reasoning behind this is that they are the perfect ladies-in-waiting, not overly intelligent, and honest. Kublai agrees and Marco immediately becomes a favored guest. Ahmed shows Marco his private tower with vultures and executes a spy via a trapdoor into a lion pit. Kukachin tells Marco that she is going to marry the King of Persia, but, having fallen in love with her, he shows her what a kiss is. A guard tells Ahmed, who vows to keep Marco out of the way. Ahmed then advises Kublai Khan to send Marco into the desert to spy on suspected rebels. Kukachin warns Marco of the deceiving Ahmed.

Cast

- Gary Cooper as Marco Polo
- Sigrid Gurie as Princess Kukachin
- Basil Rathbone as Ahmed
- George Barbier as Kublai Khan
- Binnie Barnes as Nazama
- Ernest Truex as Binguccio
- Alan Hale as Kaidu
- H.B. Warner as Chen Tsu
- Robert Greig as Chamberlain
- Ferdinand Gottschalk as Persian Ambassador
- Henry Kolker as Nicolo Polo
- Lotus Liu as Visakha
- Stanley Fields as Bayan
- Harold Huber as Toctai
- Lana Turner as Nazama's Maid

Source (edited): "http://en.wikipedia.org/wiki/The_Adventures_of_Marco_Polo"

The Battle of Midway

The Battle of Midway is a 1942 American documentary film short directed by John Ford. It is a montage of color footage of the Battle of Midway with voice overs of various narrators, including Donald Crisp, Henry Fonda, and Jane Darwell.

Plot

The film begins with a male narrator explaining where Midway Island is and its strategic importance. About five minutes into the film the format changes somewhat, with more leisurely pictures of the GIs at work on the island, and a female voice over. The female voice over takes the personality of a middle aged woman from Springfield, Ohio, who is a mother-type figure pointing out how she recognizes such and such boy from her home town. Then stock footage of the boys' mothers and sisters back home is introduced.

Abruptly the narrative turns to the battle itself with approximately five minutes dedicated to the defense of the island, the naval battle, and the aftermath. At the end the various known Japanese losses are shown (four aircraft carriers, battleships, aircraft etc.) and then brushed over with red paint.

Production notes

The film runs for 18 minutes, was distributed by 20th Century Fox, and was one of four winners of the inaugural, 1942 Academy Award for Best Documentary.

John Ford's handheld, 16mm footage of the battle was captured totally impromptu. He had been in transit on the island, roused from his bunk in the BOQ (bachelor officers' quarters) by the sounds of the battle, and started filming. Ford was wounded by enemy fire while filming the battle.

Source (edited): "http://en.wikipedia.org/wiki/The_Battle_of_Midway"

The Big Punch

The Big Punch is a 1921 Western film directed by John Ford.

Cast

- Buck Jones - Buck
- Barbara Bedford - Hope Standish
- Jack Curtis - Jed
- George Siegmann - Flash McGraw
- Jack McDonald - Friend of Jed's
- Al Fremont - Friend of Jed's
- Jennie Lee - Buck's Mother
- Edgar Jones - The Sheriff
- Irene Hunt - Dance Hall Girl
- Eleanore Gilmore

Source (edited): "http://en.wikipedia.org/wiki/The_Big_Punch"

The Black Watch

The Black Watch is a 1929 American early epic adventure drama film directed by John Ford and written by James Kevin McGuinness based on the novel *King of the Khyber Rifles* by Talbot Mundy. The film starred Victor McLaglen. The film also starred an uncredited 21-year old John Wayne as an extra and he worked in the arts and costume department also on the film.

Plot

Captain Donald King of the British Army goes to India just as World War I breaks out, convincing his comrades that he is a coward. In reality, he is on a secret mission to rescue British soldiers held prisoner there.

Cast

- Victor McLaglen as Capt. Donald Gordon King
- Myrna Loy as Yasmani
- David Rollins as Lt. Malcolm King
- Lumsden Hare as Colonel of the Black Watch
- Roy D'Arcy as Rewa Ghunga
- Mitchell Lewis as Mohammed Khan
- Cyril Chadwick as Maj. Twynes
- Claude King as General in India
- Francis Ford as Maj. MacGregor

- Walter Long as Harrim Bey
- David Torrence as Field Marshal
- Frederick Sullivan as General's Aide
- Richard Travers as Adjutant
- Pat Somerset as O'Connor, Black Watch Officer
- David Percy as Soloist, Black Watch Officer
- Joseph Diskay as Muezzin
- Joyzelle Joyner as Dancer (as Joyzelle)

Uncredited cast
- Harry Allen as Sandy
- Frank Baker as a 42nd Highlander
- Arthur Clayton as 42nd Highlander
- Gregory Gaye as a 42nd Highlander
- Mary Gordon as Sandy's Wife
- Bob Kortman as a 42nd Highlander
- Tom London as a 42nd Highlander
- Arthur Metcalfe as a 42nd Highlander
- Jack Pennick as a 42nd Highlander
- Randolph Scott as a 42nd Highlander
- Phillips Smalley as the Doctor
- Lupita Tovar in a Bit Part
- John Wayne as a 42nd Highlander

Release and acclaim

The film premiered on 8 May 1929.
Source (edited): "http://en.wikipedia.org/wiki/The_Black_Watch"

The Blue Eagle

The Blue Eagle (1926) is an action film directed by John Ford. Prints of the film exist in the Library of Congress film archive and in the UCLA Film and Television Archive.

Cast
- George O'Brien - George Darcy
- Janet Gaynor - Rose Kelly
- William Russell - Big Tim Ryan
- Margaret Livingston - Mrs. Mary Rohan
- Robert Edeson - Chaplain Regan, aka Father Joe
- Philip Ford - Limpy Darcy (as Phillip Ford)
- David Butler - Nick 'Dizzy' Galvani
- Lew Short - Sergeant Kelly
- Ralph Sipperly - Slats 'Dip' Mulligan
- Jerry Madden - Baby Tom
- Jack Herrick - 'On Da Nose' Sailor (uncredited)
- Jack Pennick - Ship's crewman (uncredited)
- Charles Sullivan - Sailor Giving George Boxing Gloves (uncredited)
- Harry Tenbrook - Bascom, a Stoker (uncredited)

Source (edited): "http://en.wikipedia.org/wiki/The_Blue_Eagle"

The Brat

The Brat is a 1931 comedy film directed by John Ford. It is based on the 1917 play by Maude Fulton. A previous silent film had been made in 1919 with Alla Nazimova. This 1931 screen version has been updated to then contemporary standards i.e. clothing, speak, topics in the news.

Background

Writer Maude Fulton was an actress as well and starred in the 1917 Broadway premiere of her own play. Two of her co-stars in the play went on to have major film careers, Lewis Stone and Edmund Lowe.

Cast
- Sally O'Neil - The Brat
- Alan Dinehart - MacMillan Forester
- Frank Albertson - Stephen Forester
- William Collier, Sr. - Judge O'Flaherty
- Virginia Cherrill - Angela
- June Collyer - Jane
- J. Farrell MacDonald - Timson, the butler
- Mary Forbes - Mrs. Forester
- Albert Gran - Bishop
- Louise Mackintosh - Lena
- Margaret Mann - Housekeeper

Source (edited): "http://en.wikipedia.org/wiki/The_Brat"

The Craving (1918 film)

The Craving is a 1918 drama film directed by John and Francis Ford. The film is considered to be lost.

Cast
- Francis Ford - Carroll Wayles
- Mae Gaston - Beulah Grey
- Peter Gerald - Ala Kasarib
- Duke Worne - Dick Wayles
- Jean Hathaway - Mrs. Wayles

Source (edited): "http://en.wikipedia.org/wiki/The_Craving_(1918_film)"

The Face on the Bar-Room Floor (1923 film)

The Face on the Bar-Room Floor is a 1923 drama film directed by John Ford. The film is considered to be lost. It was adapted from the poem of the same name by Hugh Antoine d'Arcy.

Cast
- Henry B. Walthall - Robert Stevens
- Ruth Clifford - Marion Trevor
- Ralph Emerson - Dick Von Vleck (as Walter Emerson)
- Frederick Sullivan - Thomas Waring

- Alma Bennett - Lottie
- Norval MacGregor - Governor
- Michael Dark - Henry Drew
- Gus Saville - Fisherman

Source (edited): "http://en.wikipedia.org/wiki/The_Face_on_the_Bar-Room_Floor_(1923_film)"

The Fighting Brothers

The Fighting Brothers is a 1919 short Western film directed by John Ford. The film is now considered to be lost.

Cast
- Pete Morrison - Sheriff Pete Larkin
- Hoot Gibson - Lonnie Larkin
- Yvette Mitchell - Conchita
- Jack Woods - Ben Crawly
- Duke R. Lee - Slim

Source (edited): "http://en.wikipedia.org/wiki/The_Fighting_Brothers"

The Fighting Gringo (1917 film)

The Fighting Gringo is a 1917 Western film directed by John Ford and featuring Harry Carey.

Cast
- Harry Carey - William 'Red' Saunders
- Claire Du Brey - May Smith
- George Webb - Arthur Saxon
- Rex De Rosselli - Ramon Orinez
- T. D. Crittenden - Belknap
- Tote Du Crow - Enrique
- William Steele - Jim (as Bill Gettinger)
- Vester Pegg - Pedro

Source (edited): "http://en.wikipedia.org/wiki/The_Fighting_Gringo_(1917_film)"

The Fighting Heart (1925 film)

The Fighting Heart (1925) is a drama film directed by John Ford. The film is now considered to be a lost film.

Cast
- George O'Brien - Denny Bolton
- Billie Dove - Doris Anderson
- J. Farrell MacDonald - Jerry
- Victor McLaglen - Soapy Williams
- Diana Miller - Helen Van Allen
- Bert Woodruff - Grandfather
- Francis Ford - Town Fool
- Hazel Howell - Oklahoma Kate
- Edward Peil Sr. - Flash Fogarty (as Edward Piel)
- James A. Marcus - Judge Maynard (as James Marcus)
- Frank Baker
- Harvey Clark
- Lynn Cowan
- Hank Mann
- Francis Powers

Source (edited): "http://en.wikipedia.org/wiki/The_Fighting_Heart_(1925_film)"

The Freeze-Out

The Freeze-Out is a 1921 Western film directed by John Ford and starring Harry Carey. The film is considered to be lost.

Cast
- Harry Carey - Ohio, the Stranger
- Helen Ferguson - Zoe Whipple
- Joe Harris - Headlight Whipple
- Charles Le Moyne - Denver Red
- J. Farrell MacDonald - Bobtail McGuire
- Lydia Yeamans Titus - Mrs. McGuire

Source (edited): "http://en.wikipedia.org/wiki/The_Freeze-Out"

The Fugitive (1947 film)

The Fugitive is a 1947 drama film starring Henry Fonda and directed by John Ford, based on the novel *The Power and the Glory* by Graham Greene. It was shot on location in Mexico by Mexican cinematographer Gabriel Figueroa.

Plot
A nameless priest is a fugitive in an unnamed Latin American country where religion is outlawed. Another fugitive, a murderous bandit dubbed "El Gringo", comes to town. He and a beautiful Indian woman conspire to help the priest escape. Taken to safety, he is then convinced by a police informant to return to the town on the pretense that "El Gringo" is dying and wishes to have last rites. The priest is captured and sentenced to death, but forgives the informant for betraying him. The priest's death brings an outpouring of public grief and shows the authorities that it is impossible to stamp out religion as long as it exists in people's hearts and minds.

Cast
- Henry Fonda as a fugitive
- Dolores del Río as an Indian woman
- Pedro Armendáriz as a police lieutenant
- J. Carrol Naish as a police informer
- Leo Carrillo as chief of police
- Ward Bond as El Gringo
- Robert Armstrong as police sergeant

Source (edited): "http://en.wikipedia.org/wiki/The_Fugitive_(1947_film)"

The Girl in Number 29

The Girl in Number 29 is a 1920 drama film directed by John Ford. The film is considered to be lost.

Cast
- Frank Mayo - Laurie Devon
- Elinor Fair - Barbara Devon
- Claire Anderson - Doris Williams
- Robert Bolder - Jacob Epstein
- Ruth Royce - Billie
- Ray Ripley - Ransome Shaw
- Bull Montana - Shaw's Secretary
- Arthur Hoyt - Valet
- Harry Hilliard - Rodney Bangs

Source (edited): "http://en.wikipedia.org/wiki/The_Girl_in_Number_29"

The Grapes of Wrath (film)

The Grapes of Wrath is a 1940 drama film directed by John Ford. It was based on John Steinbeck's Pulitzer Prize winning novel of the same name. The screenplay was written by Nunnally Johnson and the executive producer was Darryl F. Zanuck.

The film tells the story of the Joads, an Oklahoma family, who, after losing their farm during the Great Depression in the 1930s, become migrant workers and end up in California. The motion picture details their arduous journey across the United States as they travel to California in search of work and opportunities for the family members.

In 1989, this film was one of the first 25 films to be selected for preservation in the United States National Film Registry by the Library of Congress as being "culturally, historically, or aesthetically significant."

Plot

The film opens with Tom Joad (Henry Fonda), released from prison and hitchhiking his way back to his family farm in Oklahoma. Tom finds an itinerant ex-preacher named Jim Casy (John Carradine) sitting under a tree by the side of the road. Casy was the preacher who baptized Tom, but now Casy has "lost the spirit" and his faith (presaging his imminent conversion to communism). Casy goes with Tom to the Joad property only to find it deserted. There, they meet Muley (John Qualen) who is hiding out there. In a flashback, he describes how farmers all over the area were forced from their farms by the deed holders of the land, including a striking scene where a local boy (Irving Bacon), hired for the purpose, knocks down Muley's house with a Caterpillar tractor. Following this, Tom and Casy move on to find the Joad family at Tom's uncle John's place. His family is happy to see Tom and explain they have made plans to head for California in search of employment as their farm has been foreclosed by the bank. The large Joad family of twelve leaves at daybreak, along with Casy who decides to come along, packing everything into an old and dilapidated 1926 Hudson "Super Six" sedan adapted to serve as a truck in order to make the long journey to the promised land of California.

To reach California the Joads travel U.S. Highway 66.

The trip along Highway 66 is arduous and it soon takes a toll on the Joad family. Weak and elderly Grandpa (Charley Grapewin) is the first to die on their journey. After he dies, they pull over to the shoulder of the road, unload him, and bury him. Tom writes the circumstances surrounding the death on a page from the Family Bible and places it on the body so that if his remains were ever found his death would not be investigated as a possible homicide. They park in a camp and they meet a man, a returning migrant from California, who laughs at Pa's optimism about conditions in California and who speaks bitterly about his awful experiences in the West. He hints at what the Joads will soon find out for themselves. The family arrives at the first transient migrant campground for workers and find the camp is crowded with other starving, jobless and desperate travelers. Their truck slowly makes its way through the dirt road between the shanty houses and around the camp's hungry-faced inhabitants. Tom says, "Sure don't look none too prosperous."

After some trouble with a so-called "agitator," the Joads leave the camp in a hurry. The Joads make way to another migrant camp named the Keene Ranch. After doing some work in the fields they discover the high food prices in the company store for meat and other products. The problem is that the store is the only one in the area, by a long shot. Later they find there is a striking group of migrants in the camp and Tom wants to find out all about it. Tom goes to a secret meeting in the dark woods. The meeting is discovered and Casy is killed by one of the guards. Tom tries to defend Casy from the vicious attack and inadvertently kills the attacking guard when he retaliates.

During the altercation, Tom suffers a serious facial wound on his cheek and the camp guards realize it won't be difficult to identify him. That evening the family hides Tom under the mattresses of the truck just as guards arrive to question them and search for the killer of the guard. Tom avoids being spotted and the family successfully leaves the Keene Ranch without further incident. They drive for a while and then stop at the top of a hill when the engine overheats due to a broken fan belt; they have little gas, but decide to try coasting down the hill to some lights. The lights are from a third type of camp: Farmworkers' Wheat Patch Camp (Weedpatch in the book), a clean camp run by the Department of Agriculture. After Tom becomes personally idealized by what he has witnessed in the various camps, he describes how he plans to carry on Casy's mission in the world by fighting for social reform. Tom goes off to seek a new world, and he must leave his family to join the movement committed to social justice.

Tom Joad says:
I'll be all around in the dark. I'll be everywhere. Wherever you can look, wherever there's a fight, so hungry people can eat, I'll be there. Wherever there's a cop beatin' up a guy, I'll be there. I'll be in the way guys yell when they're mad. I'll be in the way kids laugh when they're hungry and they know supper's ready, and when the people are eatin' the stuff they raise and livin' in the houses they build, I'll be there, too.
As the family moves on again, they discuss the fear and difficulties they have had, but recognize that they have come out the other side. Ma Joad concludes the film, saying:
I ain't never gonna be scared no more. I was, though. For a while it looked as though we was beat. Good and beat. Looked like we didn't have nobody in the whole wide world but enemies. Like nobody was friendly no more. Made me feel kinda bad and scared too, like we was lost and nobody cared.... Rich fellas come up and they die, and their kids ain't no good and they die out, but we keep on coming. We're the people that live. They can't wipe us out, they can't lick us. We'll go on forever, Pa, cos we're the people.

Cast

Henry Fonda as Tom Joad.

- Henry Fonda as Tom Joad
- Russell Simpson as Pa Joad
- Jane Darwell as Ma Joad
- John Carradine as Jim Casy, former preacher
- Charley Grapewin as Grandpa William James Joad
- Zeffie Tilbury as Grandma Joad
- Frank Darien as Uncle John Joad
- Dorris Bowdon as Rose-of-Sharon "Rosasharn" Rivers
- O.Z. Whitehead as Al Joad
- Frank Sully as Noah Joad
- Darryl Hickman as Winfield Joad
- Shirley Mills as Ruthie Joad
- Eddie Quillan as Connie Rivers, husband of Rosasharn
- John Qualen as Muley Graves, neighbor in Oklahoma
- Roger Imhof as Mr. Thomas, ditch employer
- Grant Mitchell as Manager of government camp
- Charles D. Brown as Wilkie, boy lookout at dance
- John Arledge as Davis, bulldozer driver
- Ward Bond as Friendly Policeman, Bakersfield
- Eddie Waller as Proprietor

Adaptation

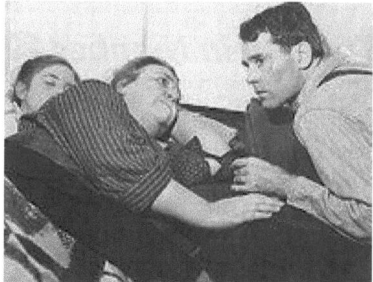

Ma and Tom Joad. Note Tom's scar on his left cheek.

The first part of the film version follows the book fairly accurately. However, the second half and the ending in particular are significantly different from the book. While the book's ending tells of the downfall and ultimate break-up of the Joad family, the film switches the entire order of sequences so that the family ends up in a "good" camp provided by the government and events turn out relatively well. Also, the novel's original ending was considered far too controversial to be included in the film. In the novel Rose-of-Sharon ("Rosasharn") Rivers (Dorris Bowdon) gives birth to a stillborn baby and later offers her milk-filled breasts to a starving man, dying in a barn. These scenes were not included in the film.

Moreover, while the film is somewhat stark it has a more optimistic and hopeful view than the novel, especially when the Joads land at the Department of Agriculture camp—the clean camp. Also, the producers tone down Steinbeck's political references in the novel like the elimination of a monologue using a land owner's description of "reds" as anybody "that wants thirty cents an hour when we're payin' twenty-five" to show that under the prevalent conditions that definition applies to every migrant worker looking for better wages. And there is also a greater emphasis on Ma Joad's pragmatic, forward-looking way of dealing with their situation despite Tom's departure and concluding in her spiritual closing "We're the people" speech.

Ivy and Sairy Wilson, who attend to Grandpa's death and travel with the Joads until they reach California, are left out of the movie. Noah's departure from the family is passed over in the movie, whereas it is shown in the book. In the book, Floyd tells Tom about how the workers were being exploited, but in the movie he does not appear until after the deputy arrives in Hooverville. Sandry, the religious fanatic who scares Rose of Sharon, is left out of the movie.

Vivian Sobchack argued that the film uses visual imagery to focus on the Joads as a family unit, whereas the novel focuses on their journey as a part of the "family of man". She points out that their farm is never shown in detail, and that the family members are never shown working in agriculture; not a single peach is shown in the entire film. This subtly serves to focus the film on the specific family, as opposed to the novel's focus on man and land together.

Production

Ma, Tom, and Pa Joad look at the hungry kids at one of the camps.

According to critic Roger Ebert, both executive producer Darryl F. Zanuck and director John Ford were odd choices to make this film because both were considered politically conservative. Zanuck was nervous about the left-wing political views of the novel, especially the ending. Due to the red-baiting common to the era, Daryl Zanuck sent private investigators to Oklahoma to help him legitimize the film. When Zanuck's investigators found that the "Okies'" predicament was indeed terrible, Zanuck was confident he could defend political attacks that the film was somehow pro-Communist. Ebert believes that World War II also helped sell the film's message, as Communism received a brief respite from American demonizing during that period.

Production on the film began on October 4, 1939, and was completed on November 16, 1939. Some of the filming locations include: McAlester, Sayre both in Oklahoma; Gallup, Laguna Pueblo, and Santa Rosa, all in New Mexico; Lamont, Needles, San Fernando Valley, all in California; Topock, Petrified Forest National Park, all in Arizona.

The film score by Alfred Newman is based on the song "Red River Valley". Additionally, the song "Goin' Down The Road Feelin' Bad" is sung in a nighttime scene at a labor camp.

The film premiered in New York City on January 24, 1940, and Los Angeles on January 27, 1940. The wide release date in the United States was March 15, 1940.

The movie was banned in the Soviet Union (USSR) by Joseph Stalin after being shown in Poland because of the depiction that even the poorest Americans could afford a car.

Reception

Critical response

Ma Joad and Tom Joad discuss Tom's future.

When released, the film was well received by the film critics, but it did have its detractors, especially because of its leftist political overtones. Film critic Frank S. Nugent, writing for *The New York Times*, liked the film's screenplay, the direction of the film and the acting. He wrote, "In the vast library where the celluloid literature of the screen is stored there is one small, uncrowded shelf devoted to the cinema's masterworks, to those films which by dignity of theme and excellence of treatment seem to be of enduring artistry, seem destined to be recalled not merely at the end of their particular year but whenever great motion pictures are mentioned. To that shelf of screen classics Twentieth Century-Fox yesterday added its version of John Steinbeck's *The Grapes of Wrath*, adapted by Nunnally Johnson, directed by John Ford and performed at the Rivoli by a cast of such uniform excellence and suitability that we should be doing its other members an injustice by saying it was 'headed' by Henry Fonda, Jane Darwell, John Carradine and Russell Simpson."

When critic Bosley Crowther retired in 1967, he named *The Grapes of Wrath* one of the best fifty films ever made. (N.B.: 40% of the works Crowther named were not American-made, so he was placing this work in a large context.)

In a film review written for *Time* magazine by its editor Whittaker Chambers, an outspoken opponent of communism, he separated his views of Steinbeck's novel from Ford's film, which he liked. Chambers wrote, "But people who go to pictures for the sake of seeing pictures will see a great one. For *The Grapes of Wrath* is possibly the best picture ever made from a so-so book...Camera craft purged the picture of the editorial rash that blotched the Steinbeck book. Cleared of excrescences, the residue is a great human story which made thousands of people, who damned the novel's phony conclusions, read it. It is the saga of an authentic U.S. farming family who lose their land. They wander, they suffer, but they endure. They are never quite defeated, and their survival is itself a triumph."

Some analysts believe the "myth of the Okies", helped created by John Steinbeck's novel, is a mistake. As such, they argue the film's story rings false. The Australian conservative commentator Keith Windschuttle, writing for *The New Criterion*, wrote, "In the film of *The Grapes of Wrath*, Steinbeck's statement that people owned their land not because they had a piece of paper but because they had been born on it, worked on it, and died on it is given to the half-crazy character Muley Graves. His sentiments, and the injustice of the dispossession behind them, resonate throughout the drama. Again, however, these remarks bear very little relationship to the real farmers of Oklahoma."

Awards
Academy Awards wins (1941)
- Best Supporting Actress, Jane Darwell as Ma Joad.
- Academy Award for Directing, John Ford.

Academy Awards nominations (1941)
- Best Actor in a Leading Role, Henry Fonda as Tom Joad.
- Best Film Editing, Robert L. Simpson.
- Best Picture, Darryl F. Zanuck and Nunnally Johnson.
- Best Sound Recording, Edmund H. Hansen.
- Best Writing Adapted Screenplay, Nunnally Johnson.

Other wins
- National Board of Review of Motion Pictures: NBR Award; Best Picture- 1940.
- New York Film Critics: NYFCC Award; Best Director, John Ford; Best Film- 1940.
- Blue Ribbon Awards, Japan: Blue Ribbon Award Best Foreign Language Film, John Ford- 1963.
- National Film Registry—1989.

American Film Institute recognition
- 100 Years...100 Movies #21
- 100 Years...100 Movies (10th Anniversary) #23
- 100 Years...100 Cheers #7
- AFI's 100 Years... 100 Heroes and Villains: Tom Joad, #12 Hero

Video and DVD
A video of the film was released in 1988 by Key Video (then a division of CBS/Fox).

Later it was released in video format on March 3, 1998 by 20th Century Fox on its Studio Classic series.

A DVD was released on April 6, 2004 by 20th Century Fox Entertainment. The DVD contains a special commentary track by scholars Joseph McBride and Susan Shillinglaw. It also includes various supplements: an A&E Network biography of Daryl F. Zanuck, outtakes, a gallery, Franklin D. Roosevelt lauds motion pictures at Academy featurette, Movietone news: three drought reports from 1934, etc.

Source (edited): "http://en.wikipedia.org/wiki/The_Grapes_of_Wrath_(film)"

The Gun Packer

The Gun Packer is a 1919 short Western film directed by John Ford.

Production
Filming began on March 25, 1919 under the working title *Out Wyoming Way*. Just two months later, *The Gun Packer* was released by Universal Studios as a 20-minute silent film on two reels. This film was reissued in August 1924.

Plot
A reformed outlaw enlists the aid of his former gunslinging companions to defend a small shepherd community from domineering cattle barons.

Cast
- Ed Jones - Sandy McLoughlin
- Pete Morrison - "Pearl Handle" Wiley
- Magda Lane - Rose McLoughlin
- Jack Woods - Pecos Smith
- Hoot Gibson - Gang Leader
- Jack Walters - Brown
- Duke R. Lee - Buck Landers
- Howard Enstaedt - Bobby McLoughlin

Source (edited): "http://en.wikipedia.org/wiki/The_Gun_Packer"

The Horse Soldiers

Horse Soldiers (2009) is also a book written by Doug Stanton
The Horse Soldiers is a 1959 DeLuxe Color war film, set in the American Civil War, directed by John Ford, starring John Wayne, William Holden and Constance Towers. The film was based on Harold Sinclair's novel of the same name.

The team of John Lee Mahin and Martin Rackin both wrote the screenplay and produced the movie.

The movie is based on the true story of Grierson's Raid and the climactic Battle of Newton's Station, led by Colonel Benjamin Grierson who, along with 1700 men, set out from northern Mississippi and rode several hundred miles behind enemy lines in April 1863 to cut the railroad between Newton's Station and Vicksburg, Mississippi. Grierson's raid was part of the Union campaign, culminating in the Battle of Vicksburg. The raid was as successful as it was daring, and remarkably bloodless. By attacking the Confederate-controlled railroad it upset the plans and troop deployments of Confederate General John C. Pemberton.

Plot summary
A Union cavalry brigade, led by Colonel John Marlowe (John Wayne), is sent on a raid behind Confederate lines to destroy a railroad and supply depot at Newton Station. Ironically, before the war, Marlowe had been a railroad building engineer. With the troop is a new regimental surgeon, Major Henry Kendall (William Holden) who seems to be constantly at odds with his commander. Kendall is torn between

the duty and the horror of war.

Complicating matters, while the unit rests at Greenbriar Plantation, Miss Hannah Hunter (Constance Towers), the plantation's mistress, and her slave Lukey (Althea Gibson) eavesdrop on a staff meeting wherein Marlowe discusses his plans. To protect the mission, Marlowe is forced to take the two women with him. Initially hostile to her Yankee captor, Miss Hunter gradually warms to him. In addition to Miss Hunter, Marlowe also has to continually contend with Col. Phil Secord who doubts Marlowe's orders and command decisions.

Several battles later, including a firefight which results in the death of Lukey, and a skirmish with Boy Cadets from a local military school (based on the real-life Battle of New Market), and with Confederate forces in pursuit, Marlowe and his command reach a bridge which must be stormed in order to access the Union lines. Dr. Kendall is forced to choose between remaining behind with some badly wounded men (and being captured with them), or leaving the men without medical care until the Confederates arrive. Marlowe and the remainder of his troop escape back to Northern lines.

Cast

- John Wayne as Colonel John Marlowe
- William Holden as Major Henry 'Hank' Kendall
- Constance Towers as Miss Hannah Hunter of Greenbriar
- Althea Gibson as Lukey, Miss Hunter's fiercely loyal black maid
- Judson Pratt as Sergeant Major Kirby
- Ken Curtis as Cpl. Wilkie
- Willis Bouchey as Col. Phil Secord
- Bing Russell as Dunker, Yankee Soldier Amputee
- O.Z. Whitehead as Otis 'Hoppy' Hopkins (medical assistant)
- Hank Worden as Deacon Clump
- Chuck Hayward as Union captain
- Denver Pyle as Jackie Jo (rebel deserter)
- Strother Martin as Virgil (rebel deserter)
- Basil Ruysdael as The Reverend (Jefferson Military Academy)
- Carleton Young as Col. Jonathan Miles, CSA
- William Leslie as Maj. Richard Gray
- William Henry as Confederate lieutenant
- Walter Reed as Union officer
- Anna Lee as Mrs. Buford
- William Forrest as Gen. Steve Hurlburt
- Ron Hagerthy as Bugler
- Russell Simpson as Acting Sheriff Henry Goodbody

Production

The Horse Soldiers was filmed on location in Natchitoches Parish Louisiana along the banks of Cane River Lake and in and around Natchez, Mississippi. John Ford cut the film's climactic battle scene short when Fred Kennedy, a veteran stuntman and bit player, was killed in a horse fall. Ford was so upset he closed the set and had to film the rest of the scene later in the San Fernando Valley. The scene with the fatal fall remains in the film.

Source (edited): "http://en.wikipedia.org/wiki/The_Horse_Soldiers"

The Hurricane (1937 film)

The Hurricane is a 1937 film set in the South Seas, directed by John Ford and produced by Samuel Goldwyn, about a Polynesian who is unjustly imprisoned. The climax features a special effects hurricane. It stars Dorothy Lamour and Jon Hall, with Mary Astor, C. Aubrey Smith, Thomas Mitchell, Raymond Massey, and John Carradine. James Norman Hall, Jon Hall's uncle, co-wrote the novel of the same name on which *The Hurricane* is based.

Plot

As a passenger ship sails by a bleak, deserted island, Dr. Kersaint (Thomas Mitchell) blows his former home a kiss. When a fellow passenger asks him about the place, he tells its tragic story, segueing into a flashback.

During the colonial era in the South Pacific, the natives of the island of Manukura are a contented lot. Terangi (Jon Hall), the first mate on an island-hopping schooner, marries Marama (Dorothy Lamour), the daughter of the chief (Al Kikume). She has a premonition and begs him not to leave, or at least take her with him on the ship's next voyage, but he makes her stay behind.

Upon reaching Tahiti, the crew goes to a bar to celebrate. When a racist white man orders them to leave, Terangi strikes him and breaks his jaw. Unfortunately, the man has strong political connections, and the governor is forced to sentence him to six months in jail, over the objections of Terangi's captain, Nagle (Jerome Cowan). Back on Manukura, Dr. Kersaint begs recently appointed local French Governor Eugene De Laage (Raymond Massey) to have Terangi brought home to serve his sentence under parole, but De Laage refuses to compromise his stern interpretation of the law, despite the pleas of Captain Nagle, Father Paul (C. Aubrey Smith), and even his own wife (Mary Astor).

Unable to bear being confined, Terangi repeatedly tries to escape, lengthening his sentence by another 16 years, much to the delight of a particularly harsh jailer (John Carradine). Finally, after eight years, Terangi succeeds in getting out, but at a terrible price: he unintentionally kills a guard. He steals a canoe and returns to Manukura after an arduous journey. At the end, he is rescued from his overturned canoe by Father Paul, who promises to remain silent.

He is reunited with Marama and a daughter (Kuulei De Clercq) he has never seen before. Chief Mehevi recommends the family hide on a tabu island, where no one will look for them. However, De Laage discovers their preparations and commandeers the schooner to hunt them down.

Terangi turns back to warn his people after he sees birds fleeing the island, an unprecedented, ominous event that Marama had dreamed about many years before. A once-in-a-lifetime hurricane strikes the island. A few, among them Dr. Kersaint and his pregnant patient, weather the disaster in a canoe, while Terangi ties his family and Madame De Laage to a stout tree. The rest drown, and the island is stripped bare.

The tree floats away. Terangi later finds a war canoe in the water, which he uses to get his party to a small island. When they spot the schooner, Terangi signals it with smoke before fleeing in the canoe with his family. Governor De Laage embraces his wife, but then spots something far away through his binoculars. Madame De Laage insists it must be a floating log; suspecting Tarangi saved his wife, after a pause, he agrees with her.

Cast

- Dorothy Lamour as Marama
- Jon Hall as Terangi
- Mary Astor as Madame Germaine De Laage
- C. Aubrey Smith as Father Paul
- Thomas Mitchell as Dr. Kersaint
- Raymond Massey as Governor Eugene De Laage
- John Carradine as Warden
- Jerome Cowan as Captain Nagle
- Al Kikume as Chief Mehevi
- Kuulei De Clercq as Tita
- Layne Tom Jr. as Mako

Awards and nominations

- Best Sound Recording - Thomas T. Moulton
- Best Supporting Actor (nomination) - Thomas Mitchell
- Best Music, Score (nomination) - Alfred Newman

Critical reception

New York Times critic Frank S. Nugent praised the climactic special effect created by James Basevi, stating, "It is a hurricane to blast you from the orchestra pit to the first mezzanine. It is a hurricane to film your eyes with spin-drift, to beat at your ears with its thunder, to clutch at your heart and send your diaphragm vaulting over your floating rib into the region just south of your tonsils." He complimented the performances of all of the principal actors with the exception of Hall, whose Terangi was described as "a competent Tarzan". Nugent also faulted the uneven pacing, but in the end, characterized the film as "one of the most thrilling spectacles the screen has provided this year." Source (edited): "http://en.wikipedia.org/wiki/The_Hurricane_(1937_film)"

The Informer (1935 film)

The Informer is a 1935 dramatic film, released by RKO. The plot concerns the underside of the Irish War of Independence, set in 1922. It stars Victor McLaglen, Heather Angel, Preston Foster, Margot Grahame, Wallace Ford, Una O'Connor and J.M. Kerrigan. The screenplay was written by Dudley Nichols from the novel *The Informer* by Liam O'Flaherty. It was directed by John Ford. The novel had previously been adapted for the 1929 British film *The Informer*.

Plot

A brutish but well-meaning Irishman, Gypo Nolan (Victor McLaglen), informs on his best friend Frankie McPhillip (Wallace Ford), who is a member of the Irish Republican Army, in order to collect the reward of £20 and sail to the United States with his girlfriend Katie Madden (Margot Grahame). The film traces his conscience-stricken emotional disintegration that eventually leads him to give himself away.

Cast

- Victor McLaglen - Gypo Nolan
- Heather Angel - Mary McPhillip
- Preston Foster - Dan Gallagher
- Margot Grahame - Katie Madden
- Wallace Ford - Frankie McPhillip
- Una O'Connor - Mrs. McPhillip
- J. M. Kerrigan - Terry
- Joe Sawyer - Bartly Mulholland (as Joseph Sauers)
- Neil Fitzgerald - Tommy Connor
- Donald Meek - Peter Mulligan
- D'Arcy Corrigan - The Blind Man
- Leo McCabe - Donahue
- Steve Pendleton - Dennis Daly (as Gaylord Pendleton)
- Francis Ford - "Judge" Flynn
- May Boley - Madame Betty

Awards and nominations

Academy Awards – 1935

The film was nominated for the Outstanding Production. McLaglen won the Best Actor for his portrayal of Gypo Nolan, beating out Charles Laughton, Clark Gable, and Franchot Tone for the better-remembered *Mutiny on the Bounty*, and Ford won for Best Director. Dudley Nichols won the Best Writing, Screenplay, but turned it down because of Union disagreements. It was the first time an Oscar was declined. The film also won the Oscar for Best Score, Max Steiner's first win.

Of the 16 (10 would have been eligible for *The Informer*) competitive awards which given at the time, *The Informer* had 6 nominations. The Academy did not award *The Informer* Best Actress for Heather Angel, Best Art Direction for Van Nest Polglase (Art Direction) and Julia Heron (Set Direction), Best Assistant Director for , Best Cinematography for Joseph H. August and Best Sound Recording for Hugh McDowell, Jr. and Robert Wise.

It was the winner of 4 Academy Awards.

The film's other awards and nominations:

- National Board of Review - Best Picture
- New York Film Critics Circle Awards - Best Film and Best Director
- Venice Film Festival - John Ford nominated for the Mussolini Cup

Adaptations in other media

The Informer was adapted as a radio play on the July 10, 1944 and October 17, 1950 episodes of The Screen Guild Theater, the March 28, 1948 episode of the Ford Theatre. On the Academy Award Theater's May 25, 1946 episode, McLaglen reprised his role.

Trivia

A presentation copy of the script, originally presented to a Seymour Roman and signed by many of the prominent cast and crew, was ostensibly found in Madison, Wisconsin among items being cleaned out of an apartment by a landlord. It was brought to the *Antiques Roadshow* and was appraised for $4,000-$5,000.

The song "The Informer", on the album Phobia by the Kinks, appears to have been inspired by the movie.
Source (edited): "http://en.wikipedia.org/wiki/The_Informer_(1935_film)"

The Iron Horse (film)

The Iron Horse is a silent film directed by John Ford in 1924. It was produced by Fox Film.

Synopsis

The film presents an idealized image of the construction of the American first transcontinental railroad. It culminates with the scene of driving of the golden spike at Promontory Summit on May 10, 1869. There is a note in the title before this scene that the two original locomotives from 1869 event are used in the film, although this is false - both engines (Union Pacific No. 119 and Jupiter) were scrapped before 1910. Of course, a romantic story with love, treachery and revenge is also here. Main stars were George O'Brien and Madge Bellamy.

There is a video version of this film, with original music composed and conducted by John Lanchbery with philharmonic orchestra from Prague. This version is softly tinted.

Cast

- George O'Brien - Davy Brandon
- Madge Bellamy - Miriam Marsh
- Charles Edward Bull - Abraham Lincoln
- Cyril Chadwick - Peter Jesson
- Will Walling - Thomas Marsh
- Francis Powers - Sgt. Slattery
- J. Farrell MacDonald - Cpl. Casey
- Jim Welch - Pvt. Schultz (as James Welch)
- George Waggner - Col. William F. 'Buffalo Bill' Cody
- Fred Kohler - Bauman
- James A. Marcus - Judge Haller (as James Marcus)
- Gladys Hulette - Ruby
- Chief John Big Tree - Cheyenne Chief (uncredited)
- Foreground - dog(black & white canine who strolled through many scenes(from property man Lefty Hough; interviewed in *Hollywood* 1980

Source (edited): "http://en.wikipedia.org/wiki/The_Iron_Horse_(film)"

The Last Hurrah (1958 film)

The Last Hurrah is a 1958 film adaptation of the novel *The Last Hurrah* by Edwin O'Connor. It was directed by John Ford and starred Spencer Tracy as a veteran mayor preparing for yet another election campaign. Tracy was nominated as Best Foreign Actor by BAFTA and won the Best Actor Award from the National Board of Review, which also presented Ford the award for Best Director.

The film tells the story of Frank Skeffington, a sentimental but iron-fisted Irish-American who is the powerful mayor of an unnamed American city. As his nephew, Adam Caulfield, follows one last no-holds-barred mayoral campaign, Skeffington and his top strategist, John Gorman, use whatever means necessary to defeat a candidate backed by civic leaders such as banker Norman Cass and newspaper editor Amos Force, the mayor's dedicated foes.

Cast

- Spencer Tracy as Mayor Frank Skeffington
- Jeffrey Hunter as Adam Caulfield
- Dianne Foster as Mave Caulfield
- Pat O'Brien as John Gorman
- Basil Rathbone as Norman Cass, Sr.
- Donald Crisp as Cardinal Martin Burke
- James Gleason as "Cuke" Gillen
- Edward Brophy as "Ditto" Boland
- John Carradine as Amos Force
- Willis Bouchey as Roger Sugrue
- Basil Ruysdael as Bishop Gardner
- Ricardo Cortez as Sam Weinberg
- Wallace Ford as Charles J. Hennessey
- Frank McHugh as Festus Garvey
- Carleton Young as Winslow
- Frank Albertson as Jack Mangan
- Bob Sweeney as Johnny Degnan
- Edmund Lowe as Johnny Byrne
- William Leslie as Dan Herlihy
- Anna Lee as Gert Minihan
- Ken Curtis as Monsignor Killian
- Jane Darwell as Delia Boylan
- O.Z. Whitehead as Norman Cass Jr.
- Arthur Walsh as Frank Skeffington Jr.

The role of Mayor Frank Skeffington was first offered to Orson Welles, as Welles recounts in Peter Bogdanovich's 1992 book *This Is Orson Welles*. However, "When the contracts were to be settled, I was away on location, and some lawyer -- if you can conceive of such a thing -- turned it down. He told Ford that the money wasn't right or the billing wasn't good enough, something idiotic like that, and when I came back to town the part had gone to Tracy."

Source (edited): "http://en.wikipedia. org/wiki/The_Last_Hurrah_(1958 _film)"

The Last Outlaw

The Last Outlaw is a 1919 short Western film directed by John Ford. Part of this film survives in the British Film Institute film archive and in the Museum of Modern Art film archive.

Cast
- Edgar Jones
- Lucille Hutton
- Richard Cummings
- Jack Walters

Source (edited): "http://en.wikipedia.org/wiki/The_Last_Outlaw"

The Long Gray Line

The Long Gray Line is a 1955 American drama film directed by John Ford based on the life of Marty Maher. Tyrone Power stars as the scrappy Irish immigrant whose 50-year career at West Point took him from dishwasher to non-commissioned officer and athletic instructor.

Maureen O'Hara, one of Ford's favorite leading ladies, plays Maher's wife and fellow immigrant, Mary O'Donnell. The film costars Ward Bond as Herman Koehler, the Master of the Sword (athletic director) and Army's head football coach (1897-1900), who first befriends Maher. Milburn Stone appears as John J. Pershing who in 1898 swears Maher into the Army. Harry Carey, Jr. makes a brief appearance as the young cadet Dwight D. Eisenhower. Philip Carey plays (fictional) Army football player and future general Chuck Dotson.

The story follows Maher's arrival at West Point and his progress from servant to beloved leader and teacher. The film also covers Maher's personal life, his romance and marriage to Mary O'Donnell, and his declining years after her death.

The phrase "The Long Gray Line" is used to describe, as a continuum, all graduates and cadets of the USMA at West Point, New York. Many of the scenes in the film were shot on location at West Point, including the "million dollar view" of the Hudson River near the parade grounds. The film was the last one in which actor Robert Francis appeared before his death at age 25.

Cast
- Tyrone Power as Martin "Marty" Maher
- Maureen O'Hara as Mary O'Donnell
- Robert Francis as James N. Sundstrom Jr.
- Donald Crisp as Old Martin
- Ward Bond as Captain Herman Koehler
- Betsy Palmer as Kitty Carter
- Philip Carey as Charles "Chuck" Dotson (as Phil Carey)
- William Leslie as James Nilsson "Red" Sundstrom
- Harry Carey Jr. as Dwight D. Eisenhower
- Patrick Wayne as Abner "Cherub" Overton
- Sean McClory as Dinny Maher
- Peter Graves as Corporal Rudolph Heinz
- Milburn Stone as Captain John J. Pershing
- Erin O'Brien-Moore as Mrs. Koehler (as Erin O'Brien Moore)
- Walter D. Ehlers as Mike Shannon
- Willis Bouchey as Major Thomas

Source (edited): "http://en.wikipedia.org/wiki/The_Long_Gray_Line"

The Long Voyage Home

The Long Voyage Home (1940) is an American drama film and directed by John Ford. It features John Wayne, Thomas Mitchell, Ian Hunter, Barry Fitzgerald, Wilfrid Lawson, John Qualen, Mildred Natwick, Ward Bond, among others.

The film was adapted by Dudley Nichols from the plays *The Moon of the Caribees*, *In The Zone*, *Bound East for Cardiff*, and *The Long Voyage Home* by Eugene O'Neill. The original plays by Eugene O'Neill were written around the time of World War I and were among his earliest plays. Ford set the story for the motion picture, however, during World War II.

The picture tells the story of the crew and passengers aboard a freighter.

Plot

The film tells the story of the crew aboard an English cargo ship named the SS *Glencairn*, during World War II, on the long voyage home from the West Indies to Baltimore and then to England. The ship carries a cargo of high-explosives.

On liberty, after a night of drinking in bars in the West Indies, the crew returns to the tramp steamer and set sail for Baltimore.

They're a motley group: a middle-aged Irishman Driscoll (Thomas Mitchell), a young Swedish ex-farmer Ole Olsen (John Wayne), the spiteful steward Cocky (Barry Fitzgerald); the brooding Lord Jim-like Englishman Smitty (Ian Hunter), and others.

After the ship picks up a load of dynamite in Baltimore, the rough seas they encounter become nerve-racking to the crew.

They're also concerned that Smitty might be a German spy because he's secretive. After they force Smitty to show them his letters from home it turns out that Smitty is an alcoholic who has run away from his family. When they near port a German plane attacks the ship, killing Smitty in a burst of machine gun fire. The rest of the crew members decide not to sign on for another voyage on the *Glencairn* and go ashore, determined to help Ole return to his family in Sweden who he has not seen in ten years. At a seedy bar Ole is tricked into taking a drugged drink and he is shanghaied aboard another ship, the *Amindra*. Driscoll and the rest of the crew rescue him from the ship, but Driscoll is accidentally left behind in the confusion. As the crew struggles back to the *Glencairn* the next morning to sign on for another voyage, they learn that the *Amindra* was sunk by German torpedoes, killing all on board.

Cast

- John Wayne as Ole Olsen
- Thomas Mitchell as Aloysius "Drisk" Driscoll
- Ian Hunter as Smitty Smith, an alias of Thomas Fenwick
- Barry Fitzgerald as Cocky
- Wilfrid Lawson as Captain
- John Qualen as Axel Swanson
- Mildred Natwick as Freda
- Ward Bond as Yank
- Arthur Shields as Donkeyman
- Joe Sawyer as Davis
- J.M. Kerrigan as Nick, Limehouse Crimp
- Rafaela Ottiano as Bella, a Tropical Woman
- Carmen Morales as Principal Spanish Girl
- Jack Pennick as Johnny Bergman
- Bob Perry as Paddy

Critical reception

Critic Bosley Crowther, film critic for *The New York Times,* liked the screenplay, the message of the film, and John Ford's direction, and wrote, "John Ford has truly fashioned a modern Odyssey—a stark and tough-fibered motion picture which tells with lean economy the never-ending story of man's wanderings over the waters of the world in search of peace for his soul...it is harsh and relentless and only briefly compassionate in its revelation of man's pathetic shortcomings. But it is one of the most honest pictures ever placed upon the screen; it gives a penetrating glimpse into the hearts of little men and, because it shows that out of human weakness there proceeds some nobility, it is far more gratifying than the fanciest hero-worshiping fare."

The staff at *Variety* magazine wrote, "Combining dramatic content of four Eugene O'Neill one-act plays, John Ford pilots adventures of a tramp steamer from the West Indies to an American port, and then across the Atlantic with cargo of high explosives. Picture is typically Fordian, his direction accentuating characterizations and adventures of the voyage."

Critic Dennis Schwartz appreciated the acting ensemble in the film and wrote, "The film was too stagebound to be effective cinema, but it scores points in its unsentimental portrait of the loser life of the lonely and desperate merchant seamen. These same misfits, who don't fit the image of heroes, nevertheless come through as men who do their duty when the chips are down and prove they will fight for their country even though it's not necessarily for patriotic reasons."

The review aggregator Rotten Tomatoes reported that 100% of critics gave the film a positive review, based on five reviews.

Awards

Wins

- New York Film Critics Circle Awards: NYFCC Award; Best Director, John Ford; 1940.

Nominations

- Academy Awards: Oscar; Best Black-and-White Cinematography, Gregg Toland; Best Special Effects, R.T. Layton (photographic), Ray Binger (photographic) and Thomas T. Moulton (sound); Best Film Editing, Sherman Todd; Best Original Score, Richard Hageman; Best Picture, John Ford; Best Screenplay Writing, Dudley Nichols; 1941.

Source (edited): "http://en.wikipedia.org/wiki/The_Long_Voyage_Home"

The Lost Patrol (1934 film)

The Lost Patrol is a 1934 war film made by RKO. It was directed and produced by John Ford, with Merian C. Cooper as executive producer and Cliff Reid as associate producer. The screenplay was by Dudley Nichols, adapted by Garrett Fort from the novel *Patrol* by Philip MacDonald. The music score was by Max Steiner and the cinematography by Harold Wenstrom. The film is a remake of a 1929 British silent film, directed and written by Walter Summers and based on the same novel, which coincidentally starred Victor McLaglen's younger brother Cyril McLaglen in the lead role.

The film starred Victor McLaglen, Boris Karloff, Wallace Ford, Reginald Denny, J.M. Kerrigan, and Alan Hale. Max Steiner received a nomination for the Academy Award for Original Music Score. It was filmed in the Algodones Dunes of California.

Plot

Scene, influenced all later remakes, depicting two main protagonists, sitting next to heavy machine gun prior to final episode.
The Lost Patrol (above left), and *Thirteen* (1936) by Mikhail Romm (right) Left to right below: *Bataan* (1943) by Tay Garnett, *Sahara* (1943) by Zoltán Korda, and *Sahara* (1995) by Brian Trenchard-Smith

During World War I, the commanding officer of a small British patrol in the Mesopotamian desert is shot and killed by an unseen Arab sniper, leaving the Sergeant (Victor McLaglen) at a loss, since he had not been informed what their mission was. He decides to try to rejoin the brigade, even though he does not know where they are or where he is.

Eventually, the eleven men reach an oasis. During the night, one of the sentries is killed, the other seriously wounded, and all their horses are stolen, leaving them stranded. One by one, the remaining men are picked off by the unseen enemy. In desperation, the Sergeant sends two men chosen by lot on foot for help, but they are caught and tortured to death, before their bodies are sent back. The pilot of a British biplane spots the survivors, but nonchalantly lands nearby and is killed before he can be warned. The men take the machine gun from the plane and set the plane on fire in a desperate bid to attract British troops. Sanders (Boris Karloff), a religious fanatic, goes mad.

In the end, only the Sergeant is left. When the Arabs finally show themselves, he manages to kill them all with the machine gun he took from the airplane, despite being wounded himself. Moments later, another British patrol arrives, attracted by the smoke from the burning plane.

Cast

- Victor McLaglen – The Sergeant
- Boris Karloff – Sanders
- Wallace Ford – Morelli
- Reginald Denny – George Brown
- J. M. Kerrigan – Quincannon
- Billy Bevan – Herbert Hale
- Alan Hale – Matlow Cook
- Brandon Hurst – Cpl. Bell
- Douglas Walton – Pearson
- Sammy Stein – Abelson
- Howard Wilson – Aviator
- Paul Hanson – Jock MacKay
- Francis Ford (uncredited) – Arab

Source (edited): "http://en.wikipedia.org/wiki/The_Lost_Patrol_(1934_film)"

The Man Who Shot Liberty Valance

The Man Who Shot Liberty Valance is a 1962 American Western film directed by John Ford and starring James Stewart and John Wayne. The black-and-white film was released by Paramount Pictures. The screenplay by James Warner Bellah and Willis Goldbeck was adapted from a short story written by Dorothy M. Johnson.

In 2007 the film was selected for preservation in the United States National Film Registry by the Library of Congress as being "culturally, historically, or aesthetically significant".

Plot

Elderly U.S. Senator Ransom "Rance" Stoddard (James Stewart) and his wife arrive by train in the small town of Shinbone, to attend the funeral of an apparent nobody in the Western United States of America. At this point the film's setting shifts back several decades to a time when a much younger Stoddard is traveling to Shinbone by stagecoach to establish a law practice.

A gang of outlaws led by gunfighter Liberty Valance (Lee Marvin) hold up the stagecoach. Stoddard is brutally beaten, left for dead and later rescued by local rancher Tom Doniphon (John Wayne). Stoddard is nursed back to health by restaurant owner Peter Ericson (John Qualen), his wife Nora (Jeanette Nolan) and daughter, Hallie (Vera Miles). It later emerges that Hallie is Doniphon's love interest.

Shinbone's townsfolk are regularly menaced by Valance and his gang. Local marshal Link Appleyard (Andy Devine) is ill prepared or unwilling to enforce the law. Doniphon is the only local prepared to challenge Valance's lawless behaviour. On one occasion Doniphon even intervenes on Stoddard's behalf when Valance publicly humiliates the inept lawyer.

Stoddard is an advocate for social justice especially by promoting education amongst Shinbone's townsfolk. He later conducts classes to teach townsfolk how to read and write. These include Hallie Ericson and Doniphon's African-American station hand Pompey (Woody Strode).

Valance is in the pay of local cattle barons intent on influencing the agenda as the territory moves towards statehood. In Shinbone, local residents hold a meeting to elect two delegates to attend a convention on statehood at the territorial capital. Valance attempts to bully the townspeople into electing him as a delegate. Eventually, Stoddard and publisher and editor of the *Shinbone Star* Dutton Peabody (Edmond O'Brien) are successful. Valance badly beats Peabody after an unflattering newspaper article is published. Sensing that Valance is out of control, Stoddard accepts a challenge to a gun duel despite his complete lack of skills. Stoddard miraculously kills Valance with one shot to the surprise of everyone including himself. Hallie responds with tearful affection and Doniphon congratulates Stoddard on his success.

Sensing that he has lost Hallie's affections, Doniphon gets drunk in the saloon and drives out Valance's men who have been calling for Stoddard to be lynched. The barman tries to tell Pompey that, as a black man, he cannot be served, to which Doniphon angrily shouts: "Who says he can't? Pour yourself a drink, Pompey". Pompey instead drags Doniphon home, where the latter burns down the house he was building in anticipation of marrying Hallie.

Stoddard is hailed as "The Man Who Shot Liberty Valance" and off the back of this achievement is nominated as the local representative to the state convention. At this point Doniphon tells Stoddard that it was he Doniphon not Stoddard that shot and killed Valance from the other side of the street.

When asked, Doniphon replies he did it to please Hallie, which he now regrets because "she's your girl now". Pushing Stoddard to go back and stand for nomination, Doniphon says, "You taught her to read and write, now give her something to read and write about!"

Stoddard returns to the convention and is chosen as representative. He marries Hallie and becomes a congressman.

The film returns to the present day with Stoddard and wife meeting their old friends at Doniphon's funeral. Stoddard is interviewed by the newspaper reporter and tells him the truth about the killing of Valance. The newspaper man burns his notes stating: "This is the West, sir. When the legend becomes fact, print the legend".

Stoddard and Hallie board the train for Washington, melancholy about the lie that led to their prosperous life. With the area becoming more and more civilized, Stoddard decides, to Hallie's delight, to retire from politics, return to the territory to set up a law practice.

Cast
- John Wayne as Tom Doniphon
- James Stewart as Ransom Stoddard
- Vera Miles as Hallie Stoddard
- Lee Marvin as Liberty Valance
- Edmond O'Brien as Dutton Peabody
- Andy Devine as Marshal Link Appleyard
- Ken Murray as Doc Willoughby
- John Carradine as Maj. Cassius Starbuckle
- Jeanette Nolan as Nora Ericson
- John Qualen as Peter Ericson
- Willis Bouchey as Jason Tully (conductor)
- Carleton Young as Maxwell Scott
- Woody Strode as Pompey
- Denver Pyle as Amos Carruthers
- Strother Martin as Floyd
- Lee Van Cleef as Reese
- Robert F. Simon as Handy Strong
- O.Z. Whitehead as Herbert Carruthers
- Paul Birch as Mayor Winder
- Joseph Hoover as Charlie Hasbrouck (reporter for 'The Star')

Production

The film was shot in black-and-white on Paramount sound stages, which was quite a contrast with Ford's other films of the period such as *The Searchers* which included vast western exteriors and colour photography. Some maintain that Paramount needed to cut costs and insisted on a lower budgeted film. Paramount executive A.C. Lyles maintains that Ford wanted to make the picture but Paramount had not the budget available. Ford then offered to make it for whatever budget they had (a puzzling scenario since Ford had two of the industry's biggest box-office attractions, James Stewart and John Wayne, lined up to work together for the first time). Lee Marvin stated at length in a filmed interview that Ford realized that the film would not be as effective shot in color because the atmosphere and use of shadows would be adversely impacted and fought to make it in black-and-white.

Although greatly admired as a filmmaker, Ford was well-known for making life difficult for his long-suffering casts, sometimes using a kind of psychological warfare on his actors to extract the most powerful performances possible. James Stewart frequently told a story about Ford embarrassing him by making him look like a racist. When asked by Ford what he thought of the appearance of Woody Strode, an African-American, in dyed grey hair, overalls and hat, Stewart remarked that "it looks a bit Uncle Remus-like". Ford then called for the crew's attention and announced that "one of our actors doesn't like Woody's costume, doesn't like Woody, and probably doesn't like Negroes". Stewart enjoyed the ribbing, and Strode himself claimed that Stewart was "one of the nicest men you'll ever meet anywhere in the world".

But Ford's famed needling sometimes was more painful. Wayne made many films with Ford, with whom he was close. However, Wayne was a frequent target of the director's venomous remarks. Strode claims that Ford "kept needling Duke [Wayne] about his failure to make it as a football player" while Strode was "a real football player". (Wayne's potential career in football had been put off by an injury.)

Ford also admonished Wayne for failing to serve in World War II while Stewart was regarded as a war hero: "How rich did you get while Jimmy was risking his life?" Wayne's failure to serve in the conflict was a source of great guilt for him.

Ford's behavior caused Wayne to take his frustrations out on Strode, who believed that they could otherwise have been friends. While filming an exterior shot on a horse-drawn cart, Wayne almost lost control of the horses and knocked Strode away when he tried to help. When the horses did stop, Wayne almost started a fight with Strode, who was much fitter. Ford gave them time to calm down, and Wayne later told Strode that they had to "work together. We both gotta be professionals". Strode blamed Ford's treatment of Wayne for the trouble, adding, "What a miserable film to make".

Music

Burt Bacharach and Hal David wrote a song called "The Man Who Shot Liberty Valance", which became a Top 10 Hit for Gene Pitney but was not used in the film. Apparently, he was not asked to record it until after the film came out. Instead, the main titles contain a stirringly hard-driving instrumental theme. The chorus of the Pitney song features two hard strikes on a drum in order to represent the shots that were fired. Jimmie Rodgers also recorded the song, in the Gene Pitney style. James Taylor covered the song on his 1985 album *That's Why I'm Here*. The Royal Guardsmen also covered the song on their 1967 album *Snoopy vs. the Red Baron*.

In certain scenes involving the character of Hallie, Ford used part of Alfred Newman's "Ann Rutledge Theme" from his earlier film *Young Mr. Lincoln*. Ford told Peter Bogdanovich in the latter's book *John Ford* that the theme evoked the same meaning, lost love, in both films.

Notable aspects

The exact location of the film's setting is unclear. There are frequent references to the "Picketwire River" in the film. The Picketwire River was a previous name for the Purgatoire River in southeastern Colorado. Even though a date was never stated, the U.S. flag in the schoolroom scene has 38 stars, placing the film after Colorado became the 38th state on August 1, 1876. Saguaro cactus are visible in parts of the film. The only section of the U.S. in which the saguaro plant is native is the Sonoran Desert in Arizona and an extremely small area of California. There is, however, no overt mention in the film of a particular territory.

Before leaving the bar to meet Ransom Stoddard, Liberty Valance wins a hand of poker with two pair, aces over eights - a set known as a dead man's hand.

Reception

The film was an instant hit when released in April 1962, thanks to its classic story and popular stars John Wayne and James Stewart. The film was nominated for Best Costume Design Edith Head, one of the few westerns to ever be nominated for the award. *The Man Who Shot Liberty Valance* has continued its popularity through repeated television broadcasts and the rental market. Along with *The Searchers*, *My Darling Clementine*, and *Stagecoach*, it is also widely considered to be one of director John Ford's best westerns and generally ranks alongside *Red River*, *The Searchers*, *The Big Trail*, and *Stagecoach* as one of John Wayne's best films.

Sergio Leone, the director of such classic Westerns as *Once Upon a Time in the West* and *The Good, the Bad and the Ugly* and one of the directors Ford influenced the most, said it was his favorite John Ford film because *"it was the only film where he (Ford) learned about something called pessimism."*

Billing

Stewart was given top billing over Wayne in the film's posters and previews, but in the film itself Wayne has top billing. Their names are displayed on pictures of signposts, one after the other, with Wayne's name shown first and his sign mounted slightly higher on its post than Stewart's. Ford remarked in an interview with Peter Bogdanovich that he made it apparent to the audience that Vera Miles' character had never gotten over Tom Doniphon because "I wanted Wayne to be the lead".

Source (edited): "http://en.wikipedia.org/wiki/The_Man_Who_Shot_Liberty_Valance"

The Outcasts of Poker Flat (1919 film)

The Outcasts of Poker Flat was a 1919 Western film directed by John Ford and featuring Harry Carey. The film is considered to be lost.

Cast

- Harry Carey - Square Shootin' Harry Lanyon/John Oakhurst
- Cullen Landis - Billy Lanyon/Tommy Oakhurst
- Gloria Hope - Ruth Watson/Sophy, the girl
- Joseph Harris - Ned Stratton
- Virginia Chester
- Duke R. Lee
- Louise Lester
- J. Farrell MacDonald
- Charles H. Mailes
- Vester Pegg
- Vic Potel

Source (edited): "http://en.wikipedia.org/wiki/The_Outcasts_of_Poker_Flat_(1919_film)"

The Phantom Riders

The Phantom Riders is a 1918 Western film directed by John Ford and featuring Harry Carey. The film is considered to be lost.

Production

Filming took place from September 7-27, 1917. Released in January 1918 as a Universal Special feature, *The Phantom Riders* was a 50-minute silent film on five reels, part of the "Cheyenne Harry" series of film featurettes. The original story was written by Henry McRae and adapted for the screen by scenarist George Hively.

Plot

Cheyenne Harry stands up to the powerful criminal boss Dave Bland who dominates Paradise Creek Valley. Attempting to save the sanctity of the vast open grazing lands, Harry also finds himself defending the honor of intimidated Molly Grant. After her father is killed and Harry is captured by Bland's thugs, it is Molly who the saves the day in the end by bringing in the US cavalry.

Cast

- Harry Carey - Cheyenne Harry
- William Steele - Dave Bland (as Bill Gettinger)
- Molly Malone - Molly Grant
- Buck Connors - 'Pebble' Grant (as Buck Connor)
- Vester Pegg - The Unknown

- Jim Corey - Foreman

Source (edited): "http://en.wikipedia.org/wiki/The_Phantom_Riders"

The Plough and the Stars (film)

The Plough and the Stars is a 1936 drama film directed by John Ford based on the play of the same name by Seán O'Casey.

Cast
- Barbara Stanwyck - Nora Clitheroe
- Preston Foster - Jack Clitheroe
- Barry Fitzgerald - Fluther Good
- Denis O'Dea - The Young Covey
- F. J. McCormick - Capt. Brennan
- Una O'Connor - Maggie Gogan
- Arthur Shields - Padraig Pearse
- Moroni Olsen - Gen. Connally
- J. M. Kerrigan - Peter Flynn
- Bonita Granville - Mollser Gogan
- Erin O'Brien-Moore - Rosie Redmond
- Neil Fitzgerald - Lt. Langon
- Robert Homans - Timmy the Barman
- Brandon Hurst - Sgt. Tinley
- Cyril McLaglen - Cpl. Stoddard
- Wesley Barry - Sniper
- D'Arcy Corrigan - Priest
- Mary Gordon - Woman at Barricades
- Doris Lloyd - Woman at Barricades

Source (edited): "http://en.wikipedia.org/wiki/The_Plough_and_the_Stars_(film)"

The Prince of Avenue A

The Prince of Avenue A (1920) is a drama film directed by John Ford. The film is considered to be lost.

Cast
- James J. Corbett - Barry O'Connor
- Richard Cummings - Patrick O'Connor
- Cora Drew - Mary O'Connor
- Frederick Vroom - William Tompkins
- Mary Warren - Mary Tompkins
- George Fisher - Regie Vanderlip
- Harry Northrup - Edgar Jones
- Mark Fenton - Father O'Toole
- John Cook - Butler (as Johnnie Cooke)
- Lydia Yeamans Titus - Housekeeper

Source (edited): "http://en.wikipedia.org/wiki/The_Prince_of_Avenue_A"

The Prisoner of Shark Island

The Prisoner of Shark Island is a 1936 film, produced by Darryl F. Zanuck, directed by John Ford, and starring Warner Baxter and Gloria Stuart.

Plot

A few short hours after the assassination of President Abraham Lincoln (Frank McGlynn Sr.), Dr. Samuel Mudd (Baxter) gives treatment to a man with a broken leg who shows up at his door. Mudd does not know that the president has been assassinated and the man who he is treating is John Wilkes Booth (Francis McDonald). Mudd is arrested for being an accessory in the assassination and is sent to prison on the Dry Tortugas, described as in the West Indies and referred to in the film as "America's own Devil's Island".

After a period of ill treatment due to his notoriety, his skills as a doctor are requested by the Commandant of the prison. The island has been in the grip of a yellow fever epidemic and the official prison doctor has fallen ill. Dr. Mudd takes charge with the blessing of the Commandant and the cooperation of the soldier guards, and the yellow jack epidemic subsides.

In the end he receives a pardon and is allowed to return home.

Historical accuracy

The film portrays Dr. Mudd as an entirely innocent victim and scapegoat, while the actual historical details of the case and his ties to Booth cast a shadow on his true innocence.

The historically accurate parts of the movie are (1) that President Abraham Lincoln was assassinated, (2) by John Wilkes Booth who sought help for a broken leg from Dr. Samuel Mudd, (3) who was subsequently tried before a military commission, found guilty of aiding Booth, and sent to an island military prison, and (4) was a hero in treating those felled in a yellow fever epidemic.

Other than this, the movie is historically inaccurate from beginning to end. Dr. Mudd's wife was named Sarah Frances, not Peggy. They had four children at the time, none of whom resembled in any way the one cute little daughter in the movie. Mrs. Mudd's father was dead, not alive and kicking as in the movie. None of the trial testimony is accurately portrayed. There is no Shark Island. Dr. Mudd was imprisoned at Fort Jefferson in the Dry Tortugas islands, Florida. One of Dr. Mudd's slaves did not follow him to prison, and try to help him escape from there. Dr. Mudd's wife and her father did not command a boat in an attempt to rescue Dr. Mudd from prison. Dr. Mudd did not engage in a running gun battle while trying to escape to his wife's fictional boat. He did try to escape a couple of months after arriving at Fort Jefferson by hiding aboard a visiting ship, but he was quickly discovered and returned to the fort. He was not placed in an underground pit as punishment for trying to escape. His punishment for trying to escape was 3 months in a large empty ground level gun room with four other prisoners. The men were allowed out of the gun room every day to work around the fort, etc.

Cast

- Warner Baxter - Dr. Samuel Alexander Mudd
- Gloria Stuart - Mrs. Peggy Mudd
- Claude Gillingwater - Col. Jeremiah Milford Dyer
- Arthur Byron - Mr. Erickson
- O. P. Heggie - Dr. MacIntyre
- Harry Carey - Commandant of Fort Jefferson
- Francis Ford - Cpl. O'Toole
- John McGuire - Lt. Lovett
- Francis McDonald - John Wilkes Booth
- Douglas Wood - Gen. Ewing
- John Carradine - Sgt. Rankin
- Joyce Kay - Martha Mudd
- Fred Kohler Jr. - Sgt. Cooper
- Ernest Whitman - 'Buck' Milford
- Paul Fix - David Herold

Adaptations

- The film inspired a radio adaptation on the "Encore Radio Theater" in 1946.
- The film also inspired the western film, *Hellgate* (1952).
- A television adaptation *The Ordeal of Dr. Mudd* was released in 1980.

Source (edited): "http://en.wikipedia.org/wiki/The_Prisoner_of_Shark_Island"

The Quiet Man

The Quiet Man is a 1952 American Technicolor romantic comedy-drama film. It was directed by John Ford and starring John Wayne, Maureen O'Hara, Victor McLaglen and Barry Fitzgerald. It was based on a 1933 *Saturday Evening Post* short story by Maurice Walsh. The film is notable for its lush photography of the Irish countryside and the long, climactic, semi-comic fist fight between Wayne and McLaglen.

Plot

Set in 1930s Ireland, Sean Thornton (John Wayne), an Irish-born American from Pittsburgh, returns to Ireland to reclaim his family's farm in Innisfree. He meets and falls in love with the fiery Mary Kate Danaher (Maureen O'Hara), the spinster sister of the bullying, loud-mouthed landowner "Red" Will Danaher (Victor McLaglen). Danaher, angry that Sean outbid him for the Thornton land adjacent to his property, initially refuses to sanction the marriage until several town locals, including the parish priest, conspire to trick him into believing that the wealthy Widow Tillane (Mildred Natwick) wants to marry him, but only if Mary Kate is no longer living in the house. After learning the truth on Sean and Mary Kate's wedding day, an enraged Will refuses to give his sister her full dowry.

Sean, unschooled in Irish customs, cares nothing about the dowry, but Mary Kate is obsessed with obtaining it, the dowry representing her independence, identity, and pride. Angered and shamed by Sean's refusal to confront her brother and demand what is legally hers, she brands him a coward, and, despite living together, they are estranged as husband and wife.

Sean is a former boxer in the United States, a heavyweight challenger known as "Trooper Thorn." After accidentally killing an opponent in the ring, Sean hung up his gloves, vowing never to fight again. The truth about Sean, however, is known only to one other person in the village, the Church of Ireland minister Rev. Playfair (Arthur Shields).

Later, in an attempt to force Sean to confront Will Danaher, Mary Kate leaves him and boards a train departing Castletown and headed to Dublin. Infuriated, Sean arrives and drags her off the train, and, followed by the townspeople, forces her to walk the five miles to Inisfree from Castletown to Will Danaher's farm. Sean demands that Will hand over her dowry and threatens to return Mary Kate to his household if Will refuses. Will finally relents and gives him the cash. Mary Kate and Sean throw it into a furnace, showing that Mary Kate never cared about the money, but only that Sean stand up for his wife. Sean and Will slug it out through the village, stop for a drink, brawl again, then become best friends. Sean regains Mary Kate's love and respect. Will Danaher and the Widow Tillane begin courting, and peace is returned to Inisfree.

Cast

- John Wayne as Sean Thornton
- Maureen O'Hara as Mary Kate Danaher
- Barry Fitzgerald as Michaleen Og Flynn
- Victor McLaglen as Squire "Red" Will Danaher
- Ward Bond as Father Peter Lonergan
- Mildred Natwick as The Widow Sarah Tillane
- Francis Ford as Dan Tobin
- Arthur Shields as Rev. Cyril Playfair
- Eileen Crowe as Mrs. Elizabeth Playfair
- Charles FitzSimons as Hugh Forbes
- James Fitzsimons (James Lilburn) (James O'Hara) as Father Paul
- Sean McClory as Owen Glynn
- Emily Eby as Mave Campbell
- Jack MacGowran as Ignatius Feeney

Cast notes

- **Charles Fitzsimons** and **James Fitzsimons** were **Maureen O'Hara**'s real life younger brothers. In this film, James was billed as **James Lilburn**, though he was later better known as James O'Hara. Barry Fitzgerald and Arthur Shields were also brothers in real life, and Francis Ford was John Ford's elder brother. Ken Curtis, later of *Gunsmoke* fame and newly married to John Ford's daughter Barbara, has a small role as the accordion player.
- Wayne brought his four children along on location, and Ford gave them parts in the important race scene in the film:

- Michael Wayne, 18 - teenage boy at races
- Mary Antonia "Toni" Wayne LaCava, 16 - teenage girl at races
- Patrick Wayne, 13 - teenage boy at races
- Melinda Wayne Munoz, 12 - young girl at races

Production

The film was something of a departure for Wayne and Ford, who were both known mostly for Westerns and other action-oriented films. It was also a departure for Republic Pictures, which backed Ford in what was considered a risky venture at the time. It was the first time the studio, known for low budget B-movies, released a film receiving an Oscar nomination, the only Best Picture nomination the studio would ever garner.

Ford read the story in 1933 and soon purchased the rights to it for $10. Republic Pictures agreed to finance the film with O'Hara and Wayne with Ford directing, only if all three agreed to film a western with Republic. All agreed and after filming *Rio Grande* they headed for Ireland to start shooting.

One of the conditions that Republic Pictures placed on John Ford was that the film came in at under two hours total running time. The finished picture was two hours and fifteen minutes. When screening the film for Republic Studio executives, Ford stopped the film at approximately two hours in: on the verge of the climactic fight between Wayne and McLaglen. Republic executives relented and allowed the film to run its full length. It was one of the few films that Republic filmed in Technicolor; most of the studio's other color films were made in a more economical process known as Trucolor.

The film employed many actors from the Irish theatre, including Barry Fitzgerald's brother, Arthur Shields, as well as extras from the Irish countryside, and it is one of the few Hollywood movies in which the Irish language can be heard.

The story is set in Innisfree, a place in Lough Gill on the Sligo-Leitrim Border made famous by poet William Butler Yeats. Many scenes for the film were actually shot in and around the village of Cong, County Mayo, on the grounds of Cong's Ashford Castle. Cong is now a wealthy small town and the castle a 5-star luxury hotel. The connections with the film have led to the area becoming a tourist attraction. In 2008 a replica of the original pub that was featured in the film was built in Cong; the pub hosts daily re-runs of the film on DVD. The Quiet Man Fan Club hold their annual general meeting in Ashford Castle each year. Other locations in the film include Thoor Ballylee, Co Galway, home of Poet W.B. Yeats for a period, Ballyglunin railway station near Tuam Co. Galway, which was filmed as Inishfree station, and various places in Connemara Co Galway and Co Mayo.

The film also presents John Ford's depiction of an idealized Irish society, with no social divisions based on class or religion. The Catholic priest Father Lonergan and the Protestant Rev. Playfair maintain a strong friendly relationship throughout the film - which represented the norm in what was then the Irish Free State. (Religious tensions occurred in the 1930s, but were the norm only in Northern Ireland). The only allusions to Anglo-Irish animosity occur after the happy couple is married and a congratulatory toast expresses the wish that they live in "freedom", and before the final donnybrook when Thornton demands his wife's dowry from Danaher. Danaher asks one of the men in the crowd if the IRA had a hand in this, to which the reply was "If it were, not a scorched stone of your fine house would be standing."

The Music

John Ford chose his friend, the eminent Hollywood composer Victor Young, to compose the score for the film. For *The Quiet Man*, Young sprinkled the soundtrack with many Irish airs such as "The Rakes of Mallow" and "The Wild Colonial Boy". One piece of music, chosen by John Ford himself, is most prominent, the melody "The Isle of Innisfree", written not by Young, but by the Irish policeman/songwriter Richard Farrelly (Dick Farrelly), who wrote it on a bus journey from County Meath to Dublin. The melody of "The Isle of Innisfree" which is first heard over the opening credit sequence with Ashford Castle in the background becomes the principal musical theme of *The Quiet Man*. The melody is reprised at least eleven times throughout the film.

The upbeat melody comedically hummed by Michaleen Og Flynn and later played on the accordion is "The Rakes of Mallow".

Public reception

The film was a financial success grossing $3.8 million in its first year of release. This was among the top ten grosses of the year. The film also inspired the 1961 Broadway musical *Donnybrook!*.

The famous kissing scene between John Wayne and Maureen O'Hara is shown in *E.T. the Extra-Terrestrial* (1982) when E.T. watches television. E.T. is interested and, moved by the scene, his telepathic contact with Elliot causes the boy to re-enact it while he is at school.

Source (edited): "http://en.wikipedia.org/wiki/The_Quiet_Man"

The Rising of the Moon (film)

The Rising of the Moon is a 1957 anthology film directed by John Ford. It consists of three episodes all set in Ireland:
- "The Majesty of the Law", based on the short story of that title by Frank O'Connor in *Bones of Contention*
- "A Minute's Wait", based on a 1914 one-act comedy by Martin J. McHugh
- "1921", based on the play *The Rising of the Moon* by Lady Gregory.

Plot

The Majesty of the Law

Police Inspector Dillon (Cyril Cusack) reluctantly sets out to see an old friend, Dan O'Flaherty (Noel Purcell). Along the way, he encounters Mickey J. (Jack MacGowran), a poitín maker who, fortunately for him, is not Dillon's target today. The inspector has the unfortunate duty of serving a warrant on O'Flaherty for striking Phelim O'Feeney (John Cowley) on the head. O'Flaherty refuses to pay the fine, as he feels he has done nothing wrong, nor will he allow O'Feeney to pay it for him. Instead, he heads off to prison.

A Minute's Wait

A train pulls up to the Dunfaill station, where Paddy Morrisey (Jimmie O'Dea) announces there will be "a minute's wait". The passengers and crew crowd into the bar for refreshments, served by Pegeen Mallory (Maureen Potter). Later, Paddy finally proposes to his longtime girlfriend Pegeen.

Mrs. Falsey (May Craig) chats with her old friend Barney Domigan (Harold Goldblatt), while her niece Mary Ann MacMahon (Maureen Connell) becomes acquainted with his son Christy (Godfrey Quigley). Domigan is on his way to arrange a marriage between Christy and a young woman with a substantial dowry. Mrs. Falsey persuades him to change his mind by informing him that the U.S. Army has awarded Mary Ann $10,000 for her father's death in battle. The young couple, unaware of this development, insist they will only marry each other.

Meanwhile, the train is repeatedly delayed, much to the befuddlement of an older English couple (Anita Sharp-Bolster and Michael Trubshawe). They are first displaced from their first class compartment to make way for a prize-winning goat. Then, they have to share their new compartment with lobsters intended for the bishop's golden jubilee. When they finally get off for some tea, they are left behind when the train finally departs.

1921

Sean Curran (Donal Donnelly) awaits his execution by the British during the "Black and Tan War". This is very unpopular with the Irish public who consider him a hero. The British warden (Joseph O'Dea) allows two "nuns" (Doreen Madden and Maureen Cusack), one of them his grieving "sister", to visit him; the false sister (an American citizen) swaps clothes and places with him. Unsuspecting Police Sergeant Michael O'Hara (Denis O'Dea) helps the pair into a waiting carriage. He notices that one is wearing high heels, but thinks little of it.

The city is immediately sealed off as the manhunt for the fugitive begins. O'Hara is assigned to watch a section of the waterfront and daydreams of what he could do with the £500 bounty. Already conflicted by divided loyalties, he is visited by his overtly nationalistic wife (Eileen Crowe). Then, Curran shows up disguised as itinerant ballad singer Jimmy Walsh. O'Hara is suspicious and has him sing; Curran chooses the patriotic "The Rising of the Moon". Despite his unconvincing rendition, he manages to slip away on a boat sent for him while O'Hara bickers with his wife. When the policeman sees Curran getting away, he starts to raise the alarm, then reconsiders and starts singing "The Rising of the Moon" himself.

Cast

- Tyrone Power - Introducer

The Majesty of the Law

- Cyril Cusack as Inspector Dillon
- Noel Purcell as Dan O'Flaherty
- Jack MacGowran as Mickey J.
- John Cowley as Phelim O'Feeney

A Minute's Wait

- Jimmy O'Dea as Paddy Morrisey, the porter
- Maureen Potter as Pegeen Mallory
- Paul Farrell as Mr. O'Brien, the train engineer
- Harold Goldblatt as Barney Domigan
- May Craig as Mrs. Falsey
- Godfrey Quigley as Christy Domigan
- Maureen Connell as Mary Ann McMahon
- Michael Trubshawe as Colonel Frobisher
- Anita Sharp-Bolster as Mrs. Frobisher

1921

- Denis O'Dea as Police Sergeant Michael O'Hara
- Eileen Crowe as Police Sergeant's Wife
- Donal Donnelly as Sean Curran
- Maureen Cusack as "Sister Mary Grace"
- Doreen Madden as "Sister Matthias"
- Joseph O'Dea as British Warden
- Maureen Delaney as Old Woman
- Frank Lawton as British Officer
- Edward Lexy as Quartermaster Sergeant

Source (edited): "http://en.wikipedia.org/wiki/The_Rising_of_the_Moon_(film)"

The Scarlet Drop

The Scarlet Drop is a 1918 Western film directed by John Ford and featuring Harry Carey. Just over 30 minutes of footage of the film now survives in the Getty Images Archive.

Cast

- Harry Carey - 'Kaintuck' Harry Ridge
- Molly Malone - Molly Calvert
- Vester Pegg - Marley Calvert
- Betty Schade - Betty Calvert
- Millard K. Wilson - Graham Lyons (as M.K. Wilson)
- Martha Mattox - Mammy
- Steve Clemente - Buck (as Steve Clemento)

Source (edited): "http://en.wikipedia.

org/wiki/The_Scarlet_Drop"

The Scrapper

The Scrapper is a 1917 short Western film directed by John Ford. The film is considered to be lost.

Cast

- John Ford - Buck, the scrapper (as Jack Ford)
- Louise Granville - Helen Dawson
- Duke Worne - Jerry Martin
- Jean Hathaway
- Martha Hayes

Source (edited): "http://en.wikipedia.org/wiki/The_Scrapper"

The Searchers (film)

The Searchers is a 1956 American Western film directed by John Ford, based on the 1954 novel by Alan Le May. It stars John Wayne as a middle-aged Civil War veteran who spends years looking for his abducted niece, along with Jeffrey Hunter as his adoptive nephew, who accompanies him.

The film was a commercial success, although it received no Academy Award nominations. It was named the Greatest American Western of all time by the American Film Institute in 2008, and it placed 12th on the American Film Institute's 2007 list of the Top 100 greatest movies of all time.

Plot

In 1868, Ethan Edwards (Wayne) returns from the American Civil War, in which he fought for the Confederacy, to the home of his brother Aaron (Walter Coy) in the wilderness of northern Texas. Wrong-doing or legal trouble in Ethan's past is suggested by his absence over the last three years, a large quantity of gold coins in his possession, a Mexican war medal that he gives to his young niece Debbie (played as a child by Natalie Wood's sister Lana Wood), and his refusal to take an oath of allegiance to the Texas Rangers.

Shortly after Ethan's arrival, cattle belonging to his neighbor Lars Jorgensen (John Qualen) are stolen, and when Captain Samuel Clayton (Ward Bond) leads Ethan and a group of Rangers to follow the trail, they discover that the theft was a ploy by Comanche Indians to draw the men away from their families. When they return home, they find the Edwards homestead in flames; Aaron, his wife Martha (Dorothy Jordan), and their son Ben (Robert Lyden) dead; and Debbie and her older sister Lucy (Pippa Scott) abducted.

After a brief funeral, the men return to pursuing the Comanches. When they find their camp, Ethan recommends an open attack, in which the girls would be killed, but Clayton insists on sneaking in. The Rangers find the camp deserted, and when they continue their pursuit, the Indians almost catch them in a trap. The Rangers fend off the Indian attack, but with too few men to ensure victory, Clayton and the posse return home, leaving Ethan to continue his search for the girls with Lucy's fiancé Brad Jorgensen (Harry Carey, Jr.) and Debbie's adopted brother Martin Pawley (Jeffrey Hunter). However, after Ethan finds Lucy brutally murdered and presumably raped in a canyon near the Comanche camp, Brad becomes enraged, rides wildly into the camp, and is killed.

Ethan and Martin search until winter, when they lose the trail. When they return to the Jorgensen ranch, Martin is enthusiastically welcomed by the Jorgensens' daughter Laurie (Vera Miles), and Ethan finds a letter waiting for him from a man named Futterman, who has information about Debbie. Ethan, who would rather travel alone, leaves without Martin the next morning, but Laurie provides Martin with a horse to catch up. At Futterman's trading post, Ethan and Martin learn that Debbie has been taken by Scar (Henry Brandon), the chief of the Nawyecka band of Comanches. A year or more later, Laurie receives a letter from Martin describing the ongoing search. In reading the letter aloud, Laurie narrates the next few scenes, in which Ethan kills Futterman for trying to steal his money, Martin accidentally buys a Comanche wife, and the two men find part of Scar's tribe killed by soldiers.

After looking for Debbie at a military fort, Ethan and Martin go to New Mexico, where a Mexican man leads them to Scar. They find Debbie, now an adolescent (Natalie Wood), living as one of Scar's wives. When she meets with the men outside the camp, she says she has become a Comanche and asks them to leave without her. However, Ethan would rather see her dead than living as an Indian. He tries to shoot her, but Martin shields her with his body and an Indian shoots Ethan with a poisoned arrow. Ethan and Martin escape to safety, where Martin saves Ethan by tending to his wound. The men then return home.

Meanwhile, Charlie McCorry (Ken Curtis) has been courting Laurie in Martin's absence. Ethan and Martin arrive home just as Charlie and Laurie's wedding is about to begin. After a fistfight between Martin and Charlie, a soldier, Lt. Greenhill (Patrick Wayne), arrives with news that Ethan's half-crazy friend Mose Harper (Hank Worden) knows where Scar is. Clayton leads his men to the Comanche camp, this time for a direct attack, but Martin is allowed to sneak in and rescue Debbie, who welcomes him. During the attack, Martin kills Scar and Ethan scalps him. When Ethan sees Debbie, Martin is unable to stop him from chasing her, but instead of killing her, Ethan carries her home. Once Debbie is safely with her family, and Martin is reunited with Laurie, Ethan walks away, alone, the cabin door closing on his receding image.

Cast

- John Wayne as Ethan Edwards
- Jeffrey Hunter as Martin Pawley
- Vera Miles as Laurie Jorgensen
- Ward Bond as Rev. Capt. Samuel Johnson Clayton
- Natalie Wood as Debbie Edwards (older)
- John Qualen as Lars Jorgensen
- Olive Carey as Mrs. Jorgensen
- Henry Brandon as Chief Cicatrice (Scar)
- Ken Curtis as Charlie McCorry
- Harry Carey, Jr. as Brad Jorgensen
- Antonio Moreno as Emilio Figueroa
- Hank Worden as Mose Harper
- Beulah Archuletta as Wild Goose Flying in the Night Sky (Look)
- Walter Coy as Aaron Edwards
- Dorothy Jordan as Martha Edwards
- Pippa Scott as Lucy Edwards
- Patrick Wayne as Lt. Greenhill
- Lana Wood as Debbie Edwards (young)

Production

The film's landscape stressed the isolation and hardship of its inhabitants.

The Searchers was produced by C.V. Whitney, directed by John Ford, and distributed by Warner Brothers. While the film was primarily set in the staked plains (Llano Estacado) of Northwest Texas, it was actually filmed in Monument Valley, Arizona/Utah. Additional scenes were filmed in Mexican Hat, Utah, in Bronson Canyon in Griffith Park, Los Angeles, and in Alberta, Canada. The film was shot in the VistaVision widescreen process. Ford originally wanted to cast Fess Parker, whose performance as Davy Crockett on television had helped spark a national craze, in the Jeffrey Hunter role, but Walt Disney, to whom Parker was under contract, refused to allow it, according to Parker's videotaped interview for the Archive of American Television. Parker notes that this was by far his single worst career reversal.

The Searchers is the first of only three films produced by Cornelius Vanderbilt Whitney's C. V. Whitney Pictures; the second being *The Missouri Traveler* in 1958 with Brandon De Wilde and Lee Marvin, the last being *The Young Land* in 1959 with Patrick Wayne and Dennis Hopper.

Historical Background

Several film critics have suggested that *The Searchers* was inspired by the 1836 kidnapping of nine-year-old Cynthia Ann Parker by Comanche warriors who raided her family's home at Fort Parker, Texas. She spent 24 years with the Comanches, married a war chief, and had three children, only to be rescued against her will by Texas Rangers. James W. Parker, Cynthia Ann's uncle, spent much of his life and fortune in what became an obsessive search for his niece, like Ethan Edwards in the film. In addition, the rescue of Cynthia Ann, during a Texas Ranger attack known as the Battle of Pease River, resembles the rescue of Debbie Edwards when the Texas Rangers attack Scar's village. Parker's story was only one of 64 real-life cases of 19th-century child abductions in Texas that author Alan Le May studied while researching the novel on which the film was based. (See captivity narrative.) Moreover, his surviving research notes indicate that the two characters who go in search of a missing girl were inspired by Brit Johnson, an African-American teamster who ransomed his captured wife and children from the Comanches in 1865. Afterward, he made at least three trips to Indian Territory and Kansas relentlessly searching for another kidnapped girl, Millie Durgan (or Durkin), until Kiowa raiders killed him in 1871.

In the 1868 report of the Indian Peace Commission an attack in 1866 on a rancher "James Box" in Texas is noted: The testimony satisfies us that since October 1865, the Kiowas, Comanches, and Apaches have substantially complied with their treaty stipulations entered into at that time at the mouth of the Little Arkansas. The only flagrant violation we were able to discover consisted in the killing of James Box and the capture of his family in western Texas about the 15th of August 1866. The alleged excuse for this act is, that they supposed an attack on Texas people would be no violation of a treaty with the United States; that as we ourselves had been at war with the people of Texas, an act of hostility on their part would not be disagreeable to us.

The ending of Le May's novel contrasts to the film's, with Debbie, called Dry-Grass-Hair by the Comanches, running from the white men and from the Indians. Marty, in one final leg of his search, finds her days later, only after she has fainted from exhaustion.

In the film, Scar's Comanche group is referred to as the Nawyecka. The more common names for this Comanche division (with whom Cynthia Ann Parker lived) are Nokoni or Nocona. Some film critics have speculated that the historical model for the cavalry attack on a Comanche village, resulting in Look's death and the taking of Comanche prisoners to a military post, was the well-known Battle of Washita River, November 27, 1868, when Lt. Col. George Armstrong Custer's 7th U.S. Cavalry attacked Black Kettle's Cheyenne camp on the Washita River (near present day Cheyenne, Oklahoma). The sequence also resembles the 1872 Battle of the North Fork of the Red River, in which the 4th Cavalry captured 124 Comanche women and children and imprisoned them at Fort Concho.

Critical interpretations

Plot

The unspoken love between Wayne's Ethan and his brother's wife Martha and his obsession with avenging her drives the film.

Many critics maintain that Ethan Edwards is in love with his brother's wife Martha. In terms of the dramatic action of the film, it is by far the strongest initiator of behavior on the lead character's part. The most startling part of this plot undercurrent is that there is not one word of dialog alluding to the relationship and feelings between Ethan and Martha, despite the importance of those factors to the plot. Every reference to this relationship is visual.

In addition, the unspoken but true passion between Ethan and Martha leads to a possible conclusion: that Debbie, who is a mere eight years old when the film begins, may be Ethan's daughter. Ethan left at the dawn of the Civil War, eight years before, and his obsessive quest to find Debbie and his refusal to let her live as an Indian, along with his gift to her of his medal, might bespeak more than mere racism and revenge and his desire to save a cousin; it might depict an absentee and guilt-ridden father's attempt to save the daughter he never raised and shamefully made by cuckolding his beloved brother.

Themes

According to critics such as Roger Ebert, Ford made an effort in this film to examine the issues of racism and genocide towards Native Americans. Ford's was not the first film to attempt this, but it was startling (particularly for later generations) in the harshness of its approach toward that racism. Ford's examination of racism starts with Edwards and his openly virulent hatred of Native Americans, opening the door for the film to examine racism as an excuse for the genocide of the Indians. Roger Ebert says: "In *The Searchers* I think Ford was trying, imperfectly, even nervously, to depict racism that justified genocide." However, Ford shows in several scenes that Ethan's racist hatred for the Indians is primarily motivated by the atrocities committed by them. Thus he is driven far more by an obsessive need for vengeance than pure unmotivated racism. Perhaps significantly, Ethan, despite his hatred of the Comanches, appears to be very learned in their language and culture. When Ethan finally encounters Scar, Ford indicates that Scar's cruelty too is motivated by revenge (*"Two sons killed by white men. For each son, I take many... scalps."*).

Natalie Wood as Debbie

The theme of miscegenation also runs through this film. Early in the film Martin earns a sour look from Ethan when he admits to being part Cherokee. Ethan says repeatedly that he will kill his niece rather than have her live "with a buck", that "living with the Comanche ain't living". Even one of the film's gentler characters, Vera Miles's Laurie, tells Martin when he explains he must protect his adoptive sister, that "Ethan will put a bullet in her brain. I tell you Martha would want him to". This outburst made clear that even the supposedly gentler characters were thoroughly tainted by racism and the fear of miscegenation. In a 1964 interview with *Cosmopolitan* magazine, Ford said: "There's some merit to the charge that the Indian hasn't been portrayed accurately or fairly in the Western, but again, this charge has been a broad generalization and often unfair. The Indian didn't welcome the white man... and he wasn't diplomatic... If he has been treated unfairly by whites in films, that, unfortunately, was often the case in real life. There was much racial prejudice in the West.

Reception

Although the film was set in Texas it was filmed in Monument Valley, Utah.

In 1989, this film was deemed "culturally, historically, or aesthetically significant" by the United States Library of Congress, and selected for preservation in its National Film Registry. *The Searchers* has been cited as one of the greatest films of all time, such as in a *Sight and Sound* poll of the greatest films ever made. In 1972, *The Searchers* was ranked 18th; in 1992, fifth; in 2002, 11th. The 2007 American Film Institute 100 Greatest American Films list ranked *The Searchers* in 12th place. In 2008, the American Film Institute named *The Searchers* as the greatest Western of all time.

American Film Institute recognition
- AFI's 100 Years... 100 Movies #96
- AFI's 100 Years... 100 Movies (10th Anniversary Edition) #12
- AFI's 10 Top 10 #1 Western

The Searchers has influenced many films. David Lean watched the film repeatedly while preparing for *Lawrence of Arabia* to help him get a sense of how to shoot a landscape. The entrance of Ethan Edwards in *The Searchers*, across a vast prairie, is echoed clearly in the across-the-desert entrance of Sherif Ali in *Lawrence of Arabia*. Sam Peckinpah referenced the aftermath of the massacre and the funeral scene in *Major Dundee*.

Martin Scorsese's *Who's That Knocking at My Door* features an extended sequence in which the two leading characters discuss the film. The film served as the inspiration for the name of the British band The Searchers.

Alex Cox's *Searchers 2.0*, while not a sequel or a remake as the title may suggest, is named for the John Ford classic. The main characters discuss films, especially westerns, including *The Searchers* throughout the film.

"That'll Be the Day," a song written by Buddy Holly and Jerry Allison, and recorded by various artists, was inspired by their viewing of this film in June 1956. John Wayne's frequently-used, world-weary catchphrase, "That'll be the day" inspired the young musicians.

Steven Spielberg's *Saving Private Ryan* pays a shot-specific homage to the famous doorway shot when the Army brings the news of the death of Private Ryan's three brothers to their mother. Source (edited): "http://en.wikipedia.org/wiki/The_Searchers_(film)"

The Secret Man

The Secret Man is a 1917 Western film directed by John Ford and featuring Harry Carey. Two of the five reels of the film survive at the Library of Congress film archive.

Production
Filming took place under the working titles *The Round Up* and *Up Against It*. The film was released by Universal Studios through a subsidiary, Universal-Butterfly, in October 1917. It was a silent film on five reels, part of the "Cheyenne Harry" series of film featurettes.

Plot
Cheyenne Harry escapes from jail and lies low, working as a hired ranch hand. When he discovers a missing child in the wilderness, however, a complex plot of honor and secrecy unfolds.

Cast
- Harry Carey - Cheyenne Harry
- Edythe Sterling - Molly (as Edith Sterling)
- J. Morris Foster - Harry Beaufort (as Morris Foster)
- Elizabeth Janes - His Child
- Vester Pegg - Bill
- William Steele (as Bill Gettinger) - The Foreman
- Steve Clemente (as Steve Clement) - Pedro, the Foreman
- Hoot Gibson - Chuck Fadden

Source (edited): "http://en.wikipedia.org/wiki/The_Secret_Man"

The Shamrock Handicap

The Shamrock Handicap (1926) is a romance film directed by John Ford. A print of the film still exists in the Museum of Modern Art film archive.

Cast
- Janet Gaynor - Lady Sheila O'Hara
- Leslie Fenton - Neil Ross
- Willard Louis - Orville Finch
- J. Farrell MacDonald - Cornelius Emmet Sarsfield 'Con' O'Shea
- Claire McDowell - Molly O'Shea
- Louis Payne - Sir Miles O'Hara
- George Harris - Jockey Bennie Ginsburg (as Georgie Harris)
- Andy Clark - 'Chesty' Morgan
- Ely Reynolds - Virus Cakes
- Thomas Delmar - Michaels (uncredited)
- Bill Elliott - Well-Wishing Villager (uncredited)
- Brandon Hurst - The Procurer of Taxes (uncredited)
- Eric Mayne - Doctor (uncredited)

Source (edited): "http://en.wikipedia.org/wiki/The_Shamrock_Handicap"

The Soul Herder

The Soul Herder is a 1917 Western film directed by John Ford and featuring Harry Carey. The film is considered to be lost.

Cast
- Harry Carey
- Molly Malone
- Hoot Gibson
- Jean Hersholt - Priest
- Fritzi Ridgeway
- Duke R. Lee
- William Steele - (as William Gettinger)
- Elizabeth James - Daughter
- Vester Pegg

Source (edited): "http://en.wikipedia.org/wiki/The_Soul_Herder"

The Sun Shines Bright

The Sun Shines Bright is a 1953 comedy film directed by John Ford, based on material taken from a series of Irvin S. Cobb stories. Ford had adapted some of the same material in 1934 in his film *Judge Priest*. That film originally had a scene depicting the lynching of Stepin Fetchit's character (and Priest's condemnation of the act), but it was cut by 20th Century Fox. The omission was one of the reasons Ford loosely reshaped the Cobb stories two decades later as *The Sun Shines Bright* for Republic Pictures, this time keeping the lynching scene (and Fetchit in a supporting role). Ford often cited *The Sun Shines Bright* as his favorite among all his films, and in later years, it was championed by critics such as Jonathan Rosenbaum and Dave Kehr, who called it "a masterpiece."

Cast

- Charles Winninger - Judge William Pittman Priest
- Arleen Whelan - Lucy Lee Lake
- John Russell - Ashby Corwin
- Stepin Fetchit - Jeff Poindexter
- Russell Simpson - Dr. Lewt Lake
- Ludwig Stössel - Herman Felsburg (as Ludwig Stossel)
- Francis Ford - Feeney (Old Backwoodsman)
- Paul Hurst - Army Sgt. Jimmy Bagby
- Mitchell Lewis - Sheriff Andy Redcliffe
- Grant Withers - Buck Ramsey
- Milburn Stone - Horace K. Maydew
- Dorothy Jordan - Lucy Lee's mother
- Elzie Emanuel - U.S. Grant 'You Ess' Woodford
- Henry O'Neill - Joe D. Habersham
- Slim Pickens - Sterling, Lanky Backwoodsman
- James Kirkwood - General Fairfield
- Ernest Whitman - Pleasant 'Uncle Plez' Woodford
- Trevor Bardette - Rufe Ramseur
- Eve March - Mallie Cramp
- Hal Baylor - Rufe Ramseur Jr.
- Jane Darwell - Mrs. Aurora Ratchitt
- Ken Williams - Maydew's Henchman
- Clarence Muse - Uncle Zack
- Mae Marsh - G.A.R. Woman at the Ball

Release

The film was entered into the 1953 Cannes Film Festival.

Herbert J. Yates, the head of Republic Pictures, had about ten minutes cut from the film against Ford's wishes. According to film historian Joseph McBride, the full 100 minute version (which did play theatrically overseas) was rediscovered when Republic inadvertently used it as a master for the 1990 videotape release. This full version is currently unavailable on home video.
Source (edited): "http://en.wikipedia.org/wiki/The_Sun_Shines_Bright"

The Tornado

The Tornado is a 1917 short Western film directed by John Ford. It was Ford's debut film as a director. The film is considered to be lost.

Cast

- John Ford - Jack Dayton (as Jack Ford)
- Jean Hathaway - Jack's mother
- Peter Gerald - Pendleton, banker from Rock River (as Pete Gerald)
- Elsie Thornton - Bess, Jack's daughter
- Duke Worne - Lesparre, the lead of Cayote gang
- John Duffy - Slick, Jack's partner

Source (edited): "http://en.wikipedia.org/wiki/The_Tornado"

The Trail of Hate

The Trail of Hate is a 1917 short drama film directed by John Ford. The film is now considered to be lost.

Cast

- John Ford - The lieutenant (as Jack Ford)
- Louise Granville
- Duke Worne
- Jack Lawton

Source (edited): "http://en.wikipedia.org/wiki/The_Trail_of_Hate"

The Village Blacksmith (film)

The Village Blacksmith is a 1922 drama film directed by John Ford. One of the eight reels survives at the UCLA Film and Television Archive, and therefore the film is considered to be lost. It was adapted from the poem of the same name by Henry Wadsworth Longfellow.

Cast

- Will Walling - John Hammond, Blacksmith (as William Walling)
- Virginia True Boardman - Mrs. John Hammond
- Virginia Valli - Alice Hammond, the Daughter
- Ida Mae McKenzie - Alice as a Child
- David Butler - Bill Hammond, the Son
- Gordon Griffith - Bill as a Child
- George Hackathorne - Johnnie Hammond, Another Son
- Pat Moore - Johnnie as a Child
- Tully Marshall - Ezra Brigham, The Squire
- Ralph Yearsley - Anson Brigham, the Son
- Henri De La Garrique - Anson as a Child
- Francis Ford - Asa Martin
- Bessie Love - Rosemary Martin, the Daughter
- Helen Field - Rosemary as a Child
- Lon Poff - Gideon Crane
- Mark Fenton - Dr. Brewster

- Cordelia Callahan - Aunt Hattie
- Caroline Rankin - Squire's Wife
- Eddie Gribbon - The Village Gossip
- Lucille Hutton - Flapper

Source (edited): "http://en.wikipedia.org/wiki/The_Village_Blacksmith_(film)"

The Wallop

The Wallop is a 1921 Western film directed by John Ford and starring Harry Carey. The film is considered to be lost.

Cast
- Harry Carey - John Wesley Pringle
- Mignonne Golden - Stella Vorhis
- William Steele - Christopher Foy (as William Gettinger)
- Charles Le Moyne - Matt Lisner
- Joe Harris - Barela
- C. E. Anderson - Applegate
- J. Farrell MacDonald - Neuces River
- Mark Fenton - Major Vorhis
- Noble Johnson - Espinol

Source (edited): "http://en.wikipedia.org/wiki/The_Wallop"

The Whole Town's Talking

The Whole Town's Talking (released in the UK as *Passport to Fame*) is a 1935 comedy film starring Edward G. Robinson as a law-abiding man who bears a striking resemblance to a killer, with Jean Arthur as his love interest. It was directed by John Ford from a screenplay by Jo Swerling and Robert Riskin based on a story by W.R. Burnett originally published in Collier's in August 1932. Burnett was also the author of the source material for Robinson's screen break-through, *Little Caesar*.

The story was remade in 1998 as the Bollywood film *Duplicate*.

Plot

Arthur Ferguson Jones (Edward G. Robinson) and Wilhelmina Clark (Jean Arthur) work at the same accounting firm. Jones turns out to look exactly like the notorious bank robber "Killer" Mannion (also Robinson) and is apprehended by the police.

After his true identity is confirmed, the district attorney gives Jones a letter identifying him, so that he can avoid the same trouble in future. Jones becomes a local celebrity and, at the behest of his boss (Paul Harvey), begins ghost-writing Mannion's "autobiography", with good-natured but street-wise Wilhelmina voluntarily acting as his "talent agent" to see that he gets paid.

Mannion decides to take advantage of his mild-mannered doppelgänger and, ultimately, leave Jones "holding the bag" for Mannion's crimes. He kidnaps Wilhelmina, Jones' visiting aunt, and a few others, and takes them back to his hideout. He instructs Jones to make a large deposit for Mannion's mother's benefit at the First National Bank, where police detectives are expecting Mannion to make another robbery attempt. Fortunately for Jones, he forgets to bring the check and unwittingly leads the police back to Mannion's hideout.

Upon his arrival, Jones is mistaken for Mannion by the waiting henchmen and quickly realizes that he is meant to be the fall guy. When Mannion returns unexpectedly, Jones orders the men to shoot Mannion. The police arrive in time to capture the rest of the gang. With Mannion dead, Jones collects a reward and takes a long-desired cruise to Shanghai with Wilhelmina.

Cast
- Edward G. Robinson as Arthur Ferguson "Jonesy" Jones / "Killer" Mannion
- Jean Arthur as Wilhelmina "Bill" Clark
- Arthur Hohl as Detective Sergeant Michael F. Boyle
- Arthur Byron as District Attorney Spencer
- Wallace Ford as Healy, 'Record' reporter
- Donald Meek as Mr. Hoyt
- Paul Harvey as J. G. Carpenter
- Edward Brophy as "Slugs" Martin (as Ed Brophy)
- Etienne Girardot as Seaver, office manager
- James Donlan as Detective Sergeant Patrick J. Howe

Cast notes
- In his autobiography, *All My Yesterdays*, Edward G. Robinson wrote of Jean Arthur, "She was whimsical without being silly, unique without being nutty, a theatrical personality who was an untheatrical person. She was a delight to work with and to know."
- Lucille Ball has a small uncredited part as a bank employee, and Francis Ford, director John Ford's older brother, appears as a newspaper reporter at the dock.

Production

The Whole Town's Talking – which had the working titles of "Jail Breaker" and "Passport to Fame". – was in production from October 24 to December 11 1934. The film incorporated some footage originally shot for Columbia's 1931 film *The Criminal Code*.

Columbia Pictures borrowed Edward G. Robinson for this film from Warner Bros. – Robinson heard about the transactions through gossip columnist Louella Parsons. At the time Robinson's career was somewhat moribund and the star was tired of playing only gangsters. He was initially opposed to the project, but become convinced after reading the script. In retrospect *The Whole Town's Talking* has been seen as a turning point for Robinson, reviving his cinematic fortunes. Along with 1938's *A Slight Case of Murder*, it was one of the few comedies Robinson made.

W.R. Burnett, who wrote the story that *The Whole Town's Talking* was based on, also wrote *Little Caesar*, which was the film that catapulted Robinson to stardom, and *High Sierra*, the film of which was a significant step for Humphrey Bogart in moving from playing gangsters to romantic lead.

Response

Film critic and historian Jean Mitry said of the film that it is "...wonderfully cut and mounted, supercharged, taut like a spring, it is a work of total perfection in its genre" and Michael Costello of All Movie Guide wrote that "Ford directs and cuts the scenes with uncharacteristic rapidity, seeming to enjoy playing off the meek clerk against the anarchic gangster."

Source (edited): "http://en.wikipedia.org/wiki/The_Whole_Town%27s_Talking"

The Wings of Eagles

The Wings of Eagles is a 1957 Metrocolor film about Frank "Spig" Wead and US Naval aviation from its inception through World War II. The film is a tribute to Wead from his friend, director John Ford.

John Wayne plays naval aviator-turned-screenwriter Wead, who wrote the story or screenplay for such films as *Hell Divers*, *Ceiling Zero*, and *They Were Expendable*.

Plot

Soon after World War I is over, "Spig" Wead, along with John Dale Price (Ken Curtis), tries to prove to the Navy the value of aviation in combat. To do this, Wead pushes the Navy to compete in racing and endurance competitions. Several races are against the US Army aviation team led by Captain Herbert Allen Hazard (based on Jimmy Doolittle - played by Kenneth Tobey).

Wead spends most of his time either flying or horsing around with his teammates, meaning that his wife Minnie, or "Min" (Maureen O'Hara), and children are ignored.

The night Wead is promoted to fighter squadron commander, he falls down a flight of stairs at home, breaks his neck and is paralyzed. When "Min" tries to console him he rejects her and the family. He will only let his Navy mates like "Jughead" Carson (Dan Dailey) and Price near him. "Jughead" visits the hospital almost daily to encourage Frank's rehabilitation. Carson also pushes "Spig" to get over his depression, try to walk, and start writing. Wead achieves some success in all three goals.

After great success in Hollywood, Wead returns to active sea duty with the Navy in World War II, developing the idea of smaller escort, or "jeep," carriers to augment the main aircraft carrier force. A heart attack sends Wead home before the war's end.

Director John Ford is himself represented in the film, in the humorously-named character of film director John Dodge, played by another Ford favorite, Ward Bond.

Cast

- John Wayne as Frank W. 'Spig' Wead
- Dan Dailey as 'Jughead' Carson
- Maureen O'Hara as Min Wead
- Ward Bond as John Dodge
- Ken Curtis as John Dale Price
- Edmund Lowe as Adm. Moffett
- Kenneth Tobey as Capt. Herbert Allen Hazard
- James Todd as Jack Travis
- Barry Kelley as Capt. Jock Clark
- Sig Ruman as Manager
- Henry O'Neill as Capt. Spear
- Willis Bouchey as Barton
- Dorothy Jordan as Rose Brentmann

Inaccuracies

Dramatic license allows for some historical inaccuracies in the film. One scene shows first the US Army around-the-world flight and then the US Navy winning the Schneider Cup. In fact the US Navy won the Schneider Cup in 1923 and the US Army embarked on the first aerial circumnavigation from March to September 1924.

Another scene shows a newsreel related to the sinking of the aircraft carrier USS Hornet (CV-8), suggesting that it had been doomed by the hit of three kamikaze suicide planes. Although two aircraft did crash into it, it also received substantial damage by bombs and torpedoes before finally being sunk by American destroyers. Additionally, the term "kamikaze" was not in use to describe suicide pilots at the time of Hornet's sinking.

Source (edited): "http://en.wikipedia.org/wiki/The_Wings_of_Eagles"

The World Moves On

The World Moves On is a 1934 drama film directed by John Ford.

Plot

The story opens 185 years ago when two families, cotton merchants in England and America, with branches in France and Prussia swear to stand by each other in a belief that a great business firmly established in four countries will be able to withstand even such another calamity as the Napoleonic Wars from which Europe is slowly recovering. Then many years later, along comes World War One and the years that follow, to test the businesses.

Cast

- Madeleine Carroll - Mrs. Warburton, 1825 / Mary Warburton Girard, 1914
- Franchot Tone - Richard Girard
- Reginald Denny - Erik von Gerhardt
- Sig Ruman - Baron von Gerhardt (as Siegfried Rumann)

- Louise Dresser - Baroness von Gerhardt
- Raul Roulien - Carlos Girard (1825) / Henri Girard (1914)
- Stepin Fetchit - Dixie
- Lumsden Hare - Gabriel Warburton (1825) / Sir John Warburton (1914)
- Dudley Digges - Mr. Manning
- Frank Melton - John Girard (1825)
- Brenda Fowler - Madame Agnes Girard (1825)
- Russell Simpson - Notary (1825)
- Walter McGrail - The Duallist (1825)
- Marcelle Corday - Madame Girard II (1914)
- Charles Bastin - Jacques Girard, the Boy (1914)
- Barry Norton - Jacques Girard (1924)
- George Irving - Charles Girard (1914)
- Ferdinand Schumann-Heink - Fritz von Gerhardt
- Georgette Rhodes - Jeanne Girard
- Claude King - Colonel Braithwaite
- Ivan F. Simpson - Clumber (as Ivan Simpson)
- Frank Moran - Sergeant Culbert, Soldier in Trench

Award

John Ford won the Award of Recommendation in 1932 for this movie.
Source (edited): "http://en.wikipedia.org/wiki/The_World_Moves_On"

They Were Expendable

They Were Expendable is a 1945 American war film directed by John Ford. The film is based on the book by William L. White, relating the story of the exploits of John D. Bulkeley, a motor torpedo boat squadron commander and Medal of Honor recipient, and Robert Kelly, a skipper, during the World War II Japanese invasion of the Philippines in 1941–1942. The characters of John Brickley (Robert Montgomery) and Rusty Ryan (John Wayne) are fictionalized name changes of the actual subjects. While both book and film depict actions which did not occur, they were believed to be real during the war and the film is noted for its verisimilitude.

Plot

A demonstration of the capabilities of PT boats is shown in Manila Bay, Philippines in December 1941. Lieutenant (junior grade) 'Rusty' Ryan (John Wayne) becomes disgusted when his superiors refuse to see the small boats as viable naval craft and is in the process of writing his request for a transfer to destroyers when news arrives of the Japanese attack on Pearl Harbor.

Ryan and Lieutenant John Brickley's (Robert Montgomery) demands for combat assignments for their squadron are frustrated for a time, but they are eventually allowed to show their capabilities. From there on, there are mostly 'action' scenes, with the exception of Ryan's romantic interludes with Army nurse Sandy Davyss (Donna Reed). With the mounting Japanese onslaught against the doomed American garrisons at Bataan and Corregidor, the squadron is sent to evacuate General Douglas MacArthur, his family, and a party of VIPs.

This done, they resume their attacks against the Japanese, who gradually whittle down the squadron. As boats are lost, their crews are sent to fight as infantry. Finally, the last boat is turned over to the Army for messenger duty. Brickley, Ryan and two ensigns are airlifted out on one of the last planes because the PT boats have proved their worth and they are needed stateside to train replacement PT boat officers and crews. The remaining enlisted men, led by Chief Mulcahey, are left behind to continue the fight with remnants of the U.S. Army and Filipino guerillas.

Cast

- Robert Montgomery as Lieutenant John Brickley
- John Wayne as Lieutenant (junior grade) 'Rusty' Ryan
- Donna Reed as 2nd Lieutenant Sandy Davyss
- Jack Holt as General Martin
- Ward Bond as BMC 'Boats' Mulcahey
- Marshall Thompson as Ensign 'Snake' Gardner
- Paul Langton as Ensign 'Andy' Andrews
- Leon Ames as Major James Morton
- Arthur Walsh as Seaman Jones
- Donald Curtis as Lieutenant (J.G.) 'Shorty' Long
- Cameron Mitchell as Ensign George Cross
- Jeff York as Ensign Tony Aiken
- Murray Alper as TM1 'Slug' Mahan
- Harry Tenbrook as 'Squarehead' Larsen SC 2c
- Jack Pennick as 'Doc'

Production

According to Ben Mankiewicz, a host of Turner Classic Movies, Ford, a well-known taskmaster, was especially hard on Wayne, who did not serve in the armed forces, during filming. When Ford had health problems, he turned to Montgomery — who had actually been a PT boat commander — to take over for him, rather than Wayne. Montgomery did so well, he was directing in his own right within a couple of years.

The film received extensive support from the Navy Department and it was shot on location on Key Biscayne, Florida, and the Florida Keys, since this region most closely approximated the South Pacific war zone. Actual U.S. Navy 80' Elco PT Boats were used throughout the filming, albeit remarked with false hull numbers that would have been in use in late 1941 and early 1942. Additional U.S. naval aircraft from nearby naval air stations were temporarily remarked and were used to simulate Japanese aircraft in the film.

Awards and honors

The film earned two Academy Award nominations, Best Visual Effects and Best Sound Recording.
Source (edited): "http://en.wikipedia.org/wiki/They_Were_Expendable"

Thieves' Gold

Thieves' Gold is a 1918 Western film directed by John Ford and featuring Harry Carey. The film is considered to be lost.

Production

Thieves' Gold was released as a Universal Special Feature in 1918. It was a 50-minute silent film on five reels, part of the "Cheyenne Harry" series of film featurettes. The original story, "Back to the Right Train" by Frederick R. Bechdolt, was adapted for the screen by scenarist George Hively. This installment of "Cheyenne Harry" won notably negative reviews by critics at the time of its release.

Plot

Cheyenne Harry tries to help his outlaw friend Padden evade arrest after Padden has drunkenly shot another man. In the end, the two mismatched friends fight it out, leaving Padden dead. In a romantic subplot, Harry's fiancée Alice leaves him, but finally returns.

Cast

- Harry Carey - Cheyenne Harry
- Molly Malone - Alice Norris
- John Cook - Uncle Larkin
- Martha Mattox - Mrs. Larkin
- Vester Pegg - Curt Simmons aka "Padden"
- Harry Tenbrook - 'Colonel' Betoski
- Helen Ware - Mrs. Savage
- L. M. Wells - Savage
- Millard K. Wilson - Undetermined Role

Source (edited): "http://en.wikipedia.org/wiki/Thieves%27_Gold"

Three Jumps Ahead

Three Jumps Ahead is a 1923 Western film directed by John Ford. The film is considered to be lost.

Cast

- Tom Mix - Steve McLean
- Alma Bennett - Annie Darrell
- Edward Peil Sr. - Buck Taggitt (as Edward Piel)
- Joseph W. Girard - John Darrell (as Joe Girard)
- Virginia True Boardman - Mrs. Darrell
- Margaret Joslin - Alicia
- Francis Ford - Ben McLean
- Harry Todd - Lige McLean
- Buster Gardner - Undetermined Role

Source (edited): "http://en.wikipedia.org/wiki/Three_Jumps_Ahead"

Three Mounted Men

Three Mounted Men is a 1918 Western film directed by John Ford and featuring Harry Carey. The film is considered to be lost.

Cast

- Harry Carey - Cheyenne Harry
- Joe Harris - Buck Masters
- Neva Gerber - Lola Masters
- Harry Carter - The Warden's Son
- Ruby Lafayette - Mrs. Masters
- Charles Hill Mailes - Warden
- Anna Townsend - Harry's Mother (as Mrs. Anna Townsend)
- Ella Hall - Undetermined Role

Source (edited): "http://en.wikipedia.org/wiki/Three_Mounted_Men"

Tobacco Road (film)

This article is about the film. For the novel, see Tobacco Road. For the play, see Tobacco Road.

Tobacco Road is a 1941 film directed by John Ford starring Charley Grapewin, Marjorie Rambeau, Gene Tierney, William Tracy and Dana Andrews. It was based on the novel of the same name by Erskine Caldwell, but the plot was rewritten for the film.

Cast

- Charley Grapewin as Jeeter Lester
- Marjorie Rambeau as Sister Bessie Rice
- Gene Tierney as Ellie May Lester
- William Tracy as Dude Lester
- Elizabeth Patterson as Ada Lester
- Dana Andrews as Capt. Tim Harmon
- Ward Bond as Lov Bensey
- Zeffie Tilbury as Grandma Lester

Production

Studios attempting to acquire the screen rights to the novel date back to 1933. RKO Pictures and Warner Bros. considered buying the rights, the first intending to assign Charles Laughton in the lead role, but were discouraged to do so. In March 1940, Columbia Pictures showed interest, but was informed that *Tobacco Road* was on the list of banned titles. Eventually, 20th Century Fox won the rights in August 1940, with RKO as its main competitor. It was believed that Fox won due to the success of *The Grapes of Wrath* (1940). They were the main preference of the copyright holders Erskine Caldwell and Jack Kirkland were reluctant to sell the rights unless the film "would be picturized honestly and fearlessly."

Initially, Henry Hull was sought from Metro-Goldwyn-Mayer to reprise the main role previously portrayed on Broadway. However, in October 1940 he was revealed to be only in consideration, along with Walter Brennan and Henry Fonda.

Much to the "immense satisfaction of the studio", John Ford was signed on as the director as early as March 1940. On production, he commented in a December 1940 interview: "We have no dirt in the picture. We've eliminated the horrible details and what we've got left is a nice dramatic story. It's a tear-jerker, with some comedy relief. What we're aiming at is to have the customers sympathize with our people and not feel disgusted." The decision was most likely a result of a November 1940 warning that "many religious folk throughout the nation may be offended by the religious aspects."

Casting was a huge problem, and it was reported that producer Darryl F. Zanuck and director Ford deliberated for weeks. Marjorie Rambeau and Gene Tierney were cast in November 1940. Most other cast members were signed on in the same month. Ford personally insisted that Charley Grapewin was cast as Jeeter, because of their previous collaboration on *The Grapes of Wrath*. To portray Dude, William Tracy had to diet and lose teeth. On his role, Tracy commented in a December 1940 interview: "It's a swell part. It's one you can sink your teeth in, if you have your teeth."

While in production, *Tobacco Road* was thought to be received as even greater than *The Grapes of Wrath*. Filming was initially set on location in Georgia, but to avoid any controversy, the studio decided in November 1940 that the film would be shot in the studio on closed sets. To further prevent the film from being banned before its release, there was no publicity.

Reception

Despite the studio's concerns over the censorship, the film was only banned in Australia for unknown reasons. Although the film received mixed reviews, it became a success at the box office, and it had grossed up to $1.9 million by 1973.

Source (edited): "http://en.wikipedia.org/wiki/Tobacco_Road_(film)"

Torpedo Squadron

Torpedo Squadron is a 1942 short documentary film shot by John Ford while he was on the island of Midway.

Source (edited): "http://en.wikipedia.org/wiki/Torpedo_Squadron"

Two Rode Together

Two Rode Together (1961) is a western film directed by John Ford, and starring James Stewart, Richard Widmark, Shirley Jones, and Linda Cristal. It was based on the novel *Comanche Captives* by Will Cook.

Plot

In the 1880s, Marshal Guthrie McCabe (Jimmy Stewart) is content to be the business and personal partner of attractive saloon owner Belle Aragon (Annelle Hayes), receiving ten percent of the profits. When relatives of Comanche captives demand that Army Major Fraser (John McIntire) free them, he uses a combination of army pressure and high pay to get the reluctant McCabe to take on the job of ransoming any he can find. He assigns Lieutenant Jim Gary (Richard Widmark) to accompany McCabe.

Marty Purcell (Shirley Jones) is haunted by the memory of her abducted younger brother Steve. She keeps a music box that belonged to him. McCabe warns her that Steve will not remember her because he was a young boy when he was taken years ago. McCabe is also promised a large reward by the wealthy stepfather of another boy.

McCabe bargains with Chief Quanah Parker (Henry Brandon) and finds four white captives. Two refuse to go back with him. One is a young woman who is married to a Comanche and has children. The other is an old woman who is believed to be dead and regards herself as being as good as dead. There is also a young man named Running Wolf, who McCabe hopes is the lost son of the wealthy family. The fourth is a Mexican woman, Elena de la Madriaga (Linda Cristal). However, she is the wife of Stone Calf (Woody Strode), a militant rival of Parker. As they leave the camp, Stone Calf tries to take back his woman and is killed by McCabe, much to Quanah Parker's satisfaction.

Running Wolf makes it very clear that he hates white people and the rich man refuses to accept him. However, a woman is convinced that Running Wolf is her lost son and claims him. Later, when she tries to cut his hair, he kills her. The settlers decide to lynch the murderer, despite Lieutenant Gary's attempt to stop them. As they drag him away, Running Wolf knocks over Marty's music box. He hears it play and recognizes the melody. Marty cannot save him and is forced to accept that nothing could have been done to bring back the brother she remembered. She accepts Gary's proposal of marriage.

Meanwhile, Elena finds herself ostracized by white society as a woman who degraded herself by submitting to a savage rather than killing herself. She decides to try her luck in California. When McCabe was reported dead, Belle quickly hired a new marshal, causing him to complain, "I didn't get a chance to vote for myself - not even once." However, he has fallen in love with Elena, so he decides to go to California with her.

Cast

- James Stewart as Marshal Guthrie McCabe
- Richard Widmark as First Lieutenant Jim Gary
- Shirley Jones as Marty Purcell
- Linda Cristal as Elena de la Madriaga
- Andy Devine as Sergeant Darius P. Posey
- John McIntire as Major Frazer
- Paul Birch as Judge Edward Purcell
- Willis Bouchey as Mr. Harry J. Wringle
- Henry Brandon as Chief Quanah Parker. Brandon also played Chief Scar, the husband of a kidnapped white woman, in the 1956 Ford masterpiece *The Searchers*.
- Harry Carey Jr. as Ortho Clegg
- Olive Carey as Mrs. Abby Frazer
- Ken Curtis as Greeley Clegg
- Chet Douglas as Deputy Ward Corby
- Annelle Hayes as Belle Aragon
- David Kent as Running Wolf
- Anna Lee as Mrs. Malaprop
- Jeanette Nolan as Mrs. Mary McCandless
- John Qualen as Ole Knudsen
- Ford Rainey as Reverend Henry Clegg
- Woody Strode as Stone Calf
- O.Z. Whitehead as Lieutenant Chase

The shoot was far from a happy one. This was not a personal project for Ford but something he did only for the money ($225,000 plus 25% of the net profits) and as a favor to Columbia Pictures head Harry Cohn, who died in 1958. Ford said he admired Cohn like "a large, brilliant serpent." The director hated the material, believing he had done a far better treatment of the theme in *The Searchers*. Even after he brought in his most trusted screenwriter Frank Nugent—the man responsible for *The Searchers* and nine other Ford classics—to fix the script, the director said it was "still crap."

Nevertheless, he took the project on and proceeded to take out his frustrations on his cast and crew. Not that this was uncharacteristic. Stewart had been warned about the director's behavior by such longtime Ford stalwarts as John Wayne and Henry Fonda (who Ford had once socked in the jaw, during the filming of *Mister Roberts*). Stewart came to learn Ford liked to keep his actors in the dark about the direction of the picture and suspicious of each other. In Andrew Sinclair's biography, *John Ford*, Stewart revealed that Ford's "direction took the form of asides. Sometimes he'd put his hand across his mouth so that others couldn't hear what he was saying to you. On *Two Rode Together* he told me to watch out for Dick Widmark because he was a good actor and that he would start stealing if I didn't watch him. Later, I learned he'd told Dick the same thing about me. He liked things to be tense."

One of the film's most renowned and impressive shots has been credited solely to Ford's mean streak. In the famous five-minute two-shot of Stewart and Widmark bantering on a river bank about money, women, and the Comanche problem, the film's downbeat comedy, misogyny, and careless attitude toward human life are summed up perfectly. Ford justified the take as a simple preference for a wide-screen two-shot over cross-cutting between close-ups of "pock-marked faces." But Stewart and others insisted Ford forced his crew to wade waist-deep into the icy river and stay there all day until the shot was completed.

The film was shot on location in Brackettville, Texas where John Wayne had filmed his *The Alamo (1960 film)*.

Relationship between Ford and Stewart

Although the movie was not a commercial success and Stewart and Ford did not make the best collaborative team, they would work for together three more times, two of those in films that took a radically different and even darker view of the western myth: *The Man Who Shot Liberty Valance* (1962) and *Cheyenne Autumn* (1964). They might not have been the best of friends on-and-off the set but they had a grudging respect for each other. The closest Ford ever came to praising Stewart was when he said, "He did a whale of a job manufacturing a character the public went for. He studied acting." Stewart wore the same hat in the film that he had worn in all his westerns with director Anthony Mann, prompting Ford to remark, "Great, now I have actors with hat approval!".

Source (edited): "http://en.wikipedia.org/wiki/Two_Rode_Together"

Up the River

Up the River (1930) is a comedy film about escaped convicts, directed by John Ford and featuring Spencer Tracy and Humphrey Bogart in their feature film debuts.

Plot

Two convicts, St. Louis (Spencer Tracy) and Dannemora Dan (Warren Hymer) befriend another convict named Steve (Humphrey Bogart), who is in love with woman's-prison inmate Judy (Claire Luce). Steve is paroled, promising Judy that he will wait for her release five months later. He returns to his hometown in New England and his mother's home. However, he is followed there by Judy's former "employer," the scam artist Frosby (Gaylord Pendleton). Frosby threatens to expose Steve's prison record if the latter refuses to go along with a scheme to defraud his neighbors. Steve goes along with it until Frosby defrauds his mother. Fortunately, at this moment St. Louis and Dannemora Dan have broken of prison and come to Steve's aid, taking away a gun he planned to use on Frosby and instead stealing back the bonds. They then return to prison in time for its annual baseball game against a rival penitentiary. The film closes with St. Louis on the pitcher's mound with his catcher,

Dannemora Dan, presumably ready to lead their team to victory.

Cast
- Spencer Tracy as Saint Louis
- Claire Luce as Judy Fields
- Warren Hymer as Dannemora Dan
- Humphrey Bogart as Steve Jordan
- William Collier, Sr. as Pop
- Joan Lawes as Jean

Casting
Tracy had starred in three shorts earlier the same year and Bogart had been an unbilled extra in a silent movie a decade before, but this is the first credited feature film for both actors. This was the only feature film that close friends Tracy and Bogart ever made together. They tried to make *The Desperate Hours* in 1955, but neither would consent to second billing, so the role intended for Tracy went to Fredric March instead.

Claire Luce (1903–1989) made very few films, but was on Broadway in many plays from 1923–1952. She should not be confused with the more famous author and playwright Clare Boothe Luce (1903–1987).

The movie was remade by 20th Century-Fox in 1938, with Preston Foster and Tony Martin respectively in the Tracy and Bogart roles.

Source (edited): "http://en.wikipedia.org/wiki/Up_the_River"

Upstream (film)

Upstream (1927) is a comedy film directed by John Ford. A "backstage drama", the movie is about a Shakespearean actor and a woman from a knife-throwing act. The film was considered to be a lost film, but in 2009 it was discovered in the New Zealand Film Archive.

It is considered the first Ford film to show some influence of German director F. W. Murnau, who began working at Fox studios in 1926. From Murnau, Ford learned how to use forced perspectives and chiaroscuro lighting, which the American director then integrated into his own more naturalistic and direct filmmaking style.

Recovery
In 2009, at the invitation of the New Zealand Film Archive, the National Film Preservation Foundation sent consultants Brian Meacham and Leslie Ann Lewis to assess its holdings of long unseen nitrate prints of American silent films. The cache was found to include astonishing treasures of at least 75 American silent films unknown to exist in the United States, including a complete tinted nitrate print of *Upstream* and a trailer for another lost John Ford feature, Strong Boy (1929). The New Zealand Film Archive turned out to have many American films that had never been shipped back to the United States after they ran in theaters. The films were supposed to be destroyed at the end of their distribution run, but some were stashed away instead. *Upstream* was considered so important that, unlike other films discovered in the New Zealand archive, it was restored in New Zealand.

20th Century Fox, a descendant company of the studio that made the movie, supported the preservation of the film in collaboration with the National Film Preservation Foundation and the Academy of Motion Picture Arts and Sciences film archive. *Upstream* received a "repremiere" at the Academy of Motion Picture Arts and Sciences in September 2010. and a European screening at Le Giornate del Cinema Muto in Pordenone Italy in October 2010. Michael Mortilla wrote music for the AMPAS screening, and Donald Sosin for the Pordenone event.

Only 15 percent of Ford's silent films are known to have survived as of 2010.

Cast
- Nancy Nash - Gertie Ryan
- Earle Foxe - Eric Brasingham
- Grant Withers - Jack La Velle
- Lydia Yeamans Titus - Miss Hattie Breckenbridge
- Raymond Hitchcock - Star Boarder
- Emile Chautard - Campbell Mandare
- Ted McNamara - Callahan and Callahan
- Sammy Cohen - Callahan and Callahan
- Judy King - Sister Team
- Lillian Worth - Sister Team
- Jane Winton - Soubrette
- Harry A. Bailey - Gus Hoffman (as Harry Bailey)
- Francis Ford - Juggler
- Ely Reynolds - Deerfoot

Source (edited): "http://en.wikipedia.org/wiki/Upstream_(film)"

Wagon Master

For the 2007 Porter Wagoner album see: Wagonmaster

Wagon Master is a 1950 Western film directed by John Ford and starring Ben Johnson, Harry Carey Jr., Joanne Dru, and Ward Bond.

Plot
Learning of their ability as experienced horsemen, Mormon Elder Wiggs (Bond), hires Travis Blue (Johnson) and Sandy Owens (Carey) to guide a small group of Mormons across the West to the San Juan River country in southeastern Utah Territory, in 1849.

Production
Ford formulated the story, and then Patrick Ford (John Ford's son) and Frank S. Nugent wrote the script. Ford and Merian C. Cooper (with Ford and Coop-

er's Argosy Pictures as production company) were co-executive producers, with Lowell J. Farrell as associate producer. Music was done by Richard Hageman, and the picture was distributed by RKO Pictures.

Ford had been shooting the film *She Wore a Yellow Ribbon* the year before (1948) in Monument Valley, near the town of Mexican Hat, Utah, close to the locations where he had also filmed *Stagecoach* (1939), *My Darling Clementine* (1946), and *Fort Apache* (1948). He wanted a different look for his next film and drove to Moab. *Wagon Master* was shot in less than a month, in 1949, for less than a million dollars. Filmed in black and white (there is a later computer-colorized version), on location, mainly northeast of the town of Moab, Utah in Professor Valley (with additional shooting at Spanish Valley southwest of Moab, and a few stage shots were done at Monument Valley). It was released on April 19, 1950.

The television series *Wagon Train* (1957-1965), starring first Ward Bond and then John McIntire, was inspired by the film. (Ford directed one episode, but was otherwise not involved with it.)
Source (edited): "http://en.wikipedia.org/wiki/Wagon_Master"

Wee Willie Winkie (film)

Wee Willie Winkie is a 1937 American adventure film directed by John Ford. The screenplay by Julien Josephson and Ernest Pascal was based on a story by Rudyard Kipling. The film stars Shirley Temple, Victor McLaglen, and Cesar Romero in a story about the British presence in nineteenth century India.

William S. Darling and David S. Hall were nominated for an Academy Award for Best Art Direction.

Plot

During the British Raj, an impoverished widow, Joyce Williams and her young daughter Priscilla, are escorted by Sergeant Donald McDuff to a remote military outpost guarding the northern frontier of India, to live with her stern father-in-law, Colonel Williams. On the way, they witness the capture of notorious rebel chief Khoda Khan.

Soon, Priscilla, nicknamed 'Wee Willie Winkie' by McDuff, wins the hearts of all the soldiers, especially her grandfather and McDuff; even Khoda Khan is touched by her visits to cheer him up in his captivity. Meanwhile, her mother is courted by Lieutenant Brandes.

Khoda Khan is rescued by his men in a daring night raid and hostilities begin. McDuff is fatally wounded while out on patrol. He passes away in the hospital, while Winkie sings "Auld Lang Syne" to him.

Winkie decides to persuade Khoda Khan to stop fighting; Mohammed-din, a soldier who is actually Khan's spy, smuggles her out of the base and takes her to the rebel mountain fortress. Khoda Khan is greatly pleased, as he knows that the colonel will bring his entire regiment in a hopeless attempt to rescue her.

However, Colonel Williams halts his force out of gunshot and walks alone to the entrance. When a couple of Khan's men start shooting at the British officer, Winkie rushes to her grandfather's side. Impressed by the colonel's courage and not wanting the little girl harmed, Khoda Khan orders his men to stop firing. He agrees to negotiate and the war ends.

Lawsuit against Graham Greene

In 1938, 20th Century Fox was awarded 3500 pounds in a lawsuit it brought against British novelist Graham Greene, who in his review of *Wee Willie Winkie* for the magazine *Night and Day* wrote: The owners of a child star are like leaseholders—their property diminishes in value every year. Time's chariot is at their back; before them acres of anonymity. Miss Shirley Temple's case, though, has a peculiar interest: infancy is her disguise, her appeal is more secret and more adult. Already two years ago she was a fancy little piece (real childhood, I think, went out after *The Littlest Rebel*). In *Captain January* she wore trousers with the mature suggestiveness of a Dietrich: her neat and well-developed rump twisted in the tap-dance: her eyes had a sidelong searching coquetry. Now in *Wee Willie Winkie*, wearing short kilts, she is completely totsy. Watch her swaggering stride across the Indian barrack-square: hear the gasp of excited expectation from her antique audience when the sergeant's palm is raised: watch the way she measures a man with agile studio eyes, with dimpled depravity. Adult emotions of love and grief glissade across the mask of childhood, a childhood that is only skin-deep. It is clever, but it cannot last. Her admirers—middle-aged men and clergymen—respond to her dubious coquetry, to the sight of her well-shaped and desirable little body, packed with enormous vitality, only because the safety curtain of story and dialogue drops between their intelligence and their desire.

Cast

- Shirley Temple as Priscilla 'Winkie' Williams
- Victor McLaglen as Sergeant Donald McDuff
- C. Aubrey Smith as Colonel Williams
- Cesar Romero as Khoda Khan
- June Lang as Joyce Williams
- Michael Whalen as Lieutenant 'Coppy' Brandes
- Willie Fung as Mohammed-din

Home media

In 2009, the film was available on videocassette and DVD in both the original black and white and in computer-colorized versions. Some editions had theatrical trailers and special features.
Source (edited): "http://en.wikipedia.org/wiki/Wee_Willie_Winkie_(film)"

What Price Glory? (1952 film)

What Price Glory is a 1952 World War I film based on a 1924 play by Maxwell Anderson and Laurence Stallings, though it used virtually none of Anderson's dialogue. Originally intended as a musical, it was filmed as a straight comedy, directed by John Ford and released by 20th Century Fox on 22 August 1952 in the U.S. It starred James Cagney and Dan Dailey as US Marines in World War I.

Plot

Flagg and Quirt are veteran United States Marines whose rivalry dates back a number of years. Flagg, now a captain, is in command of a unit on the front lines of France during World War I. Sergeant Quirt is assigned to Flagg's unit as the senior non-commissioned officer. Flagg and Quirt quickly resume their rivalry which this time takes its form over the affections of Charmaine, the daughter of the local innkeeper. However, Charmaine's desire for a husband and the reality of war give the two men a common cause.

Cast

- James Cagney as Captain Flagg
- Corinne Calvet as Charmaine
- Dan Dailey as 1st Sergeant Quirt
- William Demarest as Corporal Kiper
- Craig Hill as Lieutenant Aldrich
- Robert Wagner as Private Lewisohn
- Marisa Pavan as Nicole Bouchard
- Max Showalter as Lieutenant Moore (as Casey Adams)
- James Gleason as General Cokely
- Wally Vernon as Lipinsky
- Henri Letondal as Cognac Pete (Charmaine's father)

Source (edited): "http://en.wikipedia.org/wiki/What_Price_Glory%3F_(1952_film)"

When Willie Comes Marching Home

When Willie Comes Marching Home is a 1950 World War II comedy film directed by John Ford and starring Dan Dailey and Corinne Calvet.

Plot

William "Bill" Kluggs (Dan Dailey) is the first in his hometown of Punxatawney, West Virginia, to enlist in the Army Air Forces after the attack on Pearl Harbor, making his father Herman (William Demarest), mother Gertrude (Evelyn Varden) and girlfriend Marge Fettles (Colleen Townsend) proud. The whole town sees him off. Willie tries to become a pilot but washes out, although he proves to be so proficient at aerial gunnery that, rather than being sent to Europe to fight, he is made an instructor and assigned to a base near his hometown. After two years in the same place, he is branded a coward by the townsfolk, even though he continually requests a transfer into combat.

He finally gets his chance when a gunner on a B-17 Flying Fortress bomber gets sick and Bill is allowed to take his place. The plane takes off for England, but owing to fog, is unable to land and runs low on fuel. The crew is ordered to bail out, but Bill is asleep and doesn't parachute out of the plane until it is over German-occupied France.

He is captured immediately by the local French Resistance unit, led by the beautiful Yvonne (Corinne Calvet). While there, he sees a secret German rocket launch, which is filmed by the French. He and the film are picked up by a British torpedo boat and taken to England. There, he passes the vital information and his eyewitness confirmation on to a series of important generals, first in London and then in Washington, D.C..

During the time he is in the bomber, France, England, and Washington, he is continuously wakened when he tries to sleep, and plied with liquor as a pick-me-up or to settle motion sickness. Bill finally collapses, exhausted. He is sent to a hospital to recuperate, under strict orders not to reveal what he has done, where a doctor mistakenly puts him into a psychopath ward. When the hospital attendants believe he is crazy and try to put him in a straitjacket, Willie escapes and heads home on a freight train.

Back home, because only four days have elapsed since he left Punxatawney, his parents and girlfriend don't believe his story either. Officers from the Pentagon arrive to return him to Washington to be decorated personally by the President of the United States.

- Jimmy Lydon as Charles "Charlie" Fettles
- Lloyd Corrigan as Major Adams
- Evelyn Varden as Mrs. Gertrude Kluggs

Mae Marsh, formerly a successful silent-era actress appears in an unbilled role. Alan Hale Jr. and Vera Miles also appear in unbilled roles, early in their respective careers.

Source (edited): "http://en.wikipedia.org/wiki/When_Willie_Comes_Marching_Home"

Wild Women

Wild Women is a 1918 Western film directed by John Ford and featuring Harry Carey. The film is considered to be lost.

Production

Wild Women was a Universal Special release in February 1918. It was a silent film on five reels, part of the Western-themed "Cheyenne Harry" series of film featurettes.

Plot

Cheyenne Harry and some of his friends are mysteriously kidnapped and taken to a desert island, which turns out to be teeming with energetic native women. Harry pursues the island's appealing princess, only to be pursued himself by the less-appealing queen. In the end, the madcap hijinks are revealed to be dreams, the product of Harry's legendarily prodigious drinking.

Cast

- Harry Carey - Cheyenne Harry
- Molly Malone - The Princess
- Martha Mattox - The Queen
- Ed Jones - Pelon (as Edward Jones)
- Vester Pegg - Pegg
- E. Van Beaver - The Boss
- Wilton Taylor - Slugger Joe (as Wilfred Taylor)

Source (edited): "http://en.wikipedia.org/wiki/Wild_Women"

Women in Defense

Women in Defense is a 1941 short film produced by the Office of Emergency Management shortly before the United States entered the Second World War.

Synopsis

Opening with a shot of a statue of "the pioneer woman who helped win a continent", the film briefly outlines the way in which women could help prepare the country for the possibility of war. Among the various way women could help were:

- working in a war materials manufacturing plant
- sewing parachutes for US servicemen
- attending free lectures on how to prepare nutritious meals on presumably rationed food
- Joining the WAC or the Red Cross
- donating blood

There is also a segment on the types of costumes women would wear while engaged in war work. At the end of the film, the narrator explains women are vital to securing a healthy American home life and raising children "which has always been the first line of defense".

Source (edited): "http://en.wikipedia.org/wiki/Women_in_Defense"

Young Mr. Lincoln

Young Mr. Lincoln is a 1939 fictionalized biography/drama film about the early life of President Abraham Lincoln, directed by John Ford and starring Henry Fonda. Ford and producer Darryl F. Zanuck fought for control of the film, to the point where Ford destroyed unwanted takes for fear the studio would use them in the movie. Screenwriter Lamar Trotti was nominated for an Academy Award for Best Writing/Original Story.

In 2003, *Young Mr. Lincoln* was selected for preservation in the United States National Film Registry by the Library of Congress as being "culturally, historically, or aesthetically significant".

Plot

A family traveling through New Salem, Illinois in their wagon need groceries from Lincoln's store and the only thing of value they have that he'll take in exchange is a law book. After thoroughly reading the book, Abe opts for the law after receiving encouragement from his early, ill-fated love, Ann Rutledge (Pauline Moore). Too poor to own even a horse, he arrives in Springfield on a mule and soon establishes a law practice with friend John Stuart (Edwin Maxwell). At a July 4 celebration, a man is murdered in a brawl: the accused are two brothers. Lincoln prevents the lynching of the two accused at the jail, inter alia by telling the angry mob he really needs these clients for his first real case. Admiring his courage, Mary Todd (Marjorie Weaver) -- later to be his wife—invites Lincoln to her sister's soiree and expresses an intense interest in his future.

The key witness to the crime is a friend of the victim who claims to have seen the murder at some distance under the light of the moon. The family and Lincoln are pressured to save one of the brothers at the expense of the other's conviction. But Lincoln persists and is able, through the use of an Almanac, to demonstrate that on the night in question the moon would not have provided the light the supposed eyewitness claimed. He then drives the witness to confess that he had in fact stabbed his friend himself.

A scene cut from the film involved Lincoln meeting a very young John Wilkes Booth, his future assassin. In reality, Booth was only an infant at the time.

The film has as its basis the murder case involving William "Duff" Armstrong, which took place in 1858 at the courthouse in Beardstown, Illinois -- the only courthouse where Lincoln practiced law that is still in use.

Adaptations to Other Media

Young Mr. Lincoln was adapted as a radio play on the July 10, 1946 episode of Academy Award Theater.

The Village Theatre of Everett and Issaquah, Washington has commissioned a new musical based on the film titled *Lincoln in Love*, book and lyrics by Peter S. Kellogg and music by David Friedman.

Source (edited): "http://en.wikipedia.org/wiki/Young_Mr._Lincoln"